How To Meet Your Match Online

The Last Dating, Love, or Marriage Guide You'll Ever Need

Laura Henderson

First Printing, 2011

ISBN-13: 978-0615510781 (Lighthouse Harbor LLC)
ISBN-10: 0615510787

Printed in the United States of America

Dedication

This book is dedicated to:

My family and friends who stood by me during the breakups and heartaches, and who celebrated my eventual victory;

Emily Cressey, for showing me the true joys of entrepreneurship and encouraging me to seize my dreams;

Ciara Stewart, for never doubting I would find my Prince Charming;

Leah Dahl and Anna Batie, for not letting me go it alone;

Scott Henderson, My Match and the love of my life, for being the living proof that love is worth the struggle;

and

All the singles out there being genuine and kind to each other while trying to find Your Match - you WILL succeed!

How To Meet Your Match Online

The Last Dating, Love, or Marriage Guide You'll Ever Need

Table of Contents

Introduction:
I Found My Match
and You Can Too

My online dating story began back in 2004 at the tender age of 22. So much has happened since then that I can't even remember what finally got me online. Suffice it to say that I had just graduated from college and in my four years there my date tally was a giant goose egg. Although my lack of college dating experience provided me a great deal of anxiety (*What is wrong with me? Am I too ugly to date? Will anyone ever love me?*), I see it now as a blessing in disguise. I was able to focus on my education and avoid a lot of the traumatic heartbreak that many of my friends lived through on a daily basis.

Since it seemed life wasn't exactly dropping the perfect man at my feet, in the three months between graduation from college and the start of law school, I decided that it was time for me to take a more proactive ap-approach to my love life. I set aside a few hours, plopped myself down in front of the keyboard, signed myself up for an online dating service, prepared my profile, and sat back to wait. Waiting was all I could do, actually, because although I was on a paid site, I wasn't paying for membership. I was ready to give it a try, but not ready to plunk down sixty bucks, so I just used the free features that didn't allow actually *sending* any correspondence.

Initially, I was *thrilled* with online dating! Just opening my email inbox became a big ego boost. So many people wanted to write to me, to talk to me, to meet me! Sure, most of them weren't exactly *dateable*... but still, perhaps I wasn't still the nerdy, head-gear wearing ugly duckling from elementary school that I still pictured myself to be. Sure enough, within a couple weeks I was headed out on a date!

The first gentleman I selected to actually go out with seemed to be a bright enough guy with lots of great interests. He was 27 – five years older than I was at the time – but after the men I'd met in college, I was excited about the prospect of dating a more *mature* man. This fellow was a doctor by day (and night, actually), and an avid (former professional) mountain climber during his free time; the rest of his life was taken up by his service in the Army Reserve. "Mr. All-American," I thought, "right up my alley!"

We met at a sports bar one August evening, just a few weeks before law school started. He was already there when I walked in five minutes early. Although I was pleased by his punctuality, I was momentarily surprised by his appearance; he looked *much* older than his pictures and was likely at *least* a few inches shorter than he'd claimed. (I stand a "statuesque" six feet tall, so although I was willing to date shorter men – he'd claimed to be 5' 10" – I did have my limits.)

Although I was somewhat disappointed, I figured I was already there so I'd give him a chance and see where it went. I was so nervous I felt sick all through dinner and could only pick at my food. He talked pretty much the entire evening about his various worldly adventures, and we parted ways with a friendly hug. There were no big sparks, but I had been so nervous, I decided to give him a second chance. At the very least it was good dating experience, and at least he seemed interesting.

We saw each other again a few more times and things quickly unraveled. On a rock climbing day-trip we took together in Eastern Washington, I discovered the second lie (the first being his height): he wasn't really 27, he was 30. Then came his erratic behavior; he'd frequently be late coming to get me because he was so tired from work or Army Reserve weekends that he would fall asleep at random places (e.g. at gas stations while pumping gas). The next red flag was his temper; he once got a (well-deserved) parking ticket and was so livid that he chased the poor meter maid down the block to *literally* scream in her face about the injustice of it all.

The last straw came when I spent my precious final day of freedom before law school began helping him move into a new house. When we were unpacking his things, he disclosed how much he hated lawyers, hated laws, hated rules...

Needless to say, things didn't work out between us in the long run. Nor did they work out with the Microsoft techie I dated after him (for over a year – my mistake!), the swimming coach, the Ivy-League-educated rocket scientist, the pilot of private jets, or the slow-moving parade of other guys, none of whom was really a good fit. It always seemed like there was something wrong with the relationship – I had to "make it work" by walking on egg-shells, hiding parts of myself, or settling for behavior that seemed childish or offensive. I thought all relationships would be work like that, so I put up with way too much inappropriate and unacceptable behavior.

Maybe you've been there, too?

But here's the good news: Things *did* work out for me despite my mistakes, my initial lack of dating experience, and getting a broken heart I was afraid would never mend. And now I'm going to tell you just *how* things worked out and *why* they will work out for you too!

*   *   *

The Road To Success

The summer of 2009 was dry and one of the hottest on record in Seattle. My dating life that summer was also pretty dry, though definitely not hot. In early fall, I consoled myself with my well-rehearsed series of excuses of why I was still single and why that was okay. In truth, I did have it great. I had a successful law practice, a wonderful family, an adorable nephew, a fantastic group of friends, and I'd just bought my first home a year before. I can honestly say I was happy.

Despite all the blessings in my life, though, I still felt an emptiness alongside my happiness. I felt it on family vacations hearing the low voices of couples – best friends – through the walls at night as they got ready for bed, reminiscing about the fun we'd all had that day. I felt it watching others playing with their kids. I felt it at weddings, watching through joyful tears as friends and family members pledged their lives to another.

One day that fall my sister disclosed to me that her New Year's Resolution that year had been to help me find love. She said that she knew I was ready to find love, and she wanted the happiness she had with her husband and family for me. That made *at least* two of us! There was something about this confession of hers that awakened something inside me. I don't know whether it was the surprise that someone had been making a dedicated (behind the scenes) effort for nearly a year to help me find My Match or an amalgamation of everything else going on in my life, but when she revealed that secret, something just *clicked*. My mind opened, and I accepted that there was a different reality for my life than the one I had been living so many years.

My childhood dream of having a husband and family of my own had been fading over the years like an old picture yellowing in a window. In its place was the vision of woman working hard at her job, being a good friend and aunt, and finding happiness where it arose in my life. It wasn't the picture I wanted, but it was the picture that was coming to be. But with this shift in my thinking, the original picture of the life I *truly* wanted came back into sharp relief. I decided that I was willing to spend whatever it took, or climb whatever mountain was set in front of me, if only it would help me to find the love of my life, My Match.

This was truly a turning point.

Once I *chose* a different reality for myself, it was as if I was handed the key to every locked door I had ever encountered in my dating life. Instead of working harder, everything became easier than ever before. I began exploring exactly who it was that I saw in my future – who I saw myself becoming, and who would stand next to me in that future I wanted to run toward that very moment.

My process of exploration and discovery (the process upon which my business is founded) led me quickly and efficiently toward My Match. In the next couple months, I dated two men who weren't right and moved on from them quickly. In just *three months from my epiphany*, I went out on my first date with the man who would become my husband. Less than a year later, we were engaged. And just six months after that? Married! My joy is immeasurable, and for the first time, I'm actually *living* the life I'd only dreamed about before.

How My Success Will Lead To Yours

I knew I had to share my knowledge and recipe for success with others because *everyone deserves to be this happy!* One month after my engagement, I left my job as an attorney at a Seattle law firm to pursue my big dream of founding a company, Meet Your Match Online, designed around the principles that led to my own dating success, and to the success of others with whom I've consulted who employ them.

Using my background in psychology and legal practice "finessing" the English language, I work with each client to get to the heart of why each might not be succeeding in his or her own journey toward finding love, to help each one to determine who he or she desired, and to create the perfect plan and profile to attract His or Her Match. In this book, I present these same strategies I use with my clients to you to learn and implement from the comfort of your living room.

I'll tell you how to find Your Match, but it will be up to you to put the work in to make it happen for you. Use my experience in reviewing thousands of online dating profiles to learn exactly what to do, and what *not* to do. Work through the process step-by-step and you'll learn to find love *faster and with less effort* than you ever thought possible.

Over the years I learned more than I realized about dating online and off, and the myriad of obstacles that can stand in the way of dating success if we let them. From never going out on dates, to staying with the absolute *wrong* people way too long, there are a million places to go wrong.

I read countless relationship and "how to" marriage guides in an attempt to ensure I was doing everything humanly possible to find My Match. As I devoured these books, I become more and more disheartened reading how many of them had to date hundreds of men (some even claim to have dated over a hundred in a single year) to find the right person. I hated first dates – even good first dates I found stressful and angst-ridden. I thought, *"If that's what it takes, I'll never find love!"* I was ready to give up right then and there!

However, I am VERY happy to be able to tell you that *dating hundreds of men does NOT have to be your reality!* In fact, I'll show you how being *selective* with your choices will help you find love faster. Not only will you narrow in and date people who are more likely to be right for you, but you'll get rid of the wrong ones sooner and be *available* when Mr. or Miss Right comes along!

Dating is a numbers game, but it's more about the number of good potential matches you get yourself in front of than just the number of people you actually go out on a date with. While you may have to get outside your comfort zone and "kiss a few frogs" along the path I lay out for you, it certainly won't have to be the whole swamp.

So if what you've been doing hasn't been working for you then it's time to make a different choice! You will see how easy it will be to achieve EXACTLY the results you're looking for with a few simple techniques that you will learn and be able to implement as you go. All you have to do is *decide to change!*

This process can change your life – and it will when YOU are ready. For now, just commit to reading this book. If it resonates with you, commit to giving my methods a try. It will be easy to follow the steps I set out for you. As you work through them, keep in mind that these methods work EVERY DAY for people *just like you*!

I cannot tell you *where* you will find Your Match, but I CAN tell you that he or she is out there. I can also tell you *how* to find Your Match – though it's going to require some work on your part. And most important, I can tell you that IT IS WORTH IT! Don't give up on love. You owe it to your Match not to give up on finding him or her, not to stay in relationships with the wrong people, and to do everything you can to be emotionally ready and available when he or she comes along.

So sit down, get a nice big cup of tea and your coziest blanket, and relax as you read this book. Enjoy the leisure, because as soon as you're done, you'll be chomping at the bit to GET OUT THERE and find Your Match, just like I did!

PART ONE: PREPARATION

Before setting out the tasks you'll need to accomplish and sending you marching off in search of Your Match, let's start with a bit of background on the world of online dating to ensure you're well-prepared for this journey.

In Part One you will learn: (1) why success in online dating isn't as easy as slapping up a profile, (2) why you can finally overcome your preconceived notions about online dating, (3) how to avoid online dating burn out, (4) the number one reason why daters fail – and how to avoid setting yourself up for failure – and (5) how to date online or offline *safely!*

Chapter 1: Why You Need This Book

Nearly everyone over the age of ten can grab a knife, slice a frog's chest open, and start dissecting; that doesn't mean you want a fifth-grader on your transplant team.

Similarly, any Tom, Dick, or Tammy with computer access can sign up for an online dating service, but it doesn't mean his or her profile will accurately portray who he is, who she's looking for, or even remotely come close attracting the right person to date.

The ease with which one can sign up for online dating services provides a false sense of confidence and security. Just as you can go online to post photographs from a great party you'll later regret when they're circulating the office, and type your social security number into the *wrong* website, it's also too easy to slap a dating profile together and launch it into the internet's atmosphere.

Without any forethought, daters will throw their hastily-prepared profiles up on various dating sites. Months, and often years, pass by as users' hearts become heavy with frustration while their wallets become light on funds. They have set forth a version of themselves that even they wouldn't want to date if they went back and looked at it. That's why it's so important to do things right the first time around.

The market for online dating services is booming. Research suggests that in the U.S. alone, consumers will spend $932 million on online dating in 2011.[1] The nearly $1 billion spent annually on online dating sites doesn't begin to count the real cost to online daters, which includes wasted time and money squandered on terrible first dates, transportation, new clothes, haircuts, car detailing, spa services, and more.[2]

> *The nearly $1 billion spent annually on online dating sites doesn't begin to count the real cost to online daters: wasted time, money, and energy!*

In my business, I meet all kinds: people who have struggled for years dating online, people who haven't been on a date in decades (despite a stated strong desire to get a date), people who go out on more than five dates a month (each one more terrible than the last), and even

---

[1] Retrieved March 29, 2011: "U.S. Online Dating Market to Reach $932 Million in 2011". Tekrati. http://industry.tekrati.com/research/8487/. Citation dated 2007-02-12.
[2] Participants surveyed about money spent on first dates frequently listed these line item costs; survey conducted by Lighthouse Harbor LLC in March 2011.

those who are so frustrated they've given up dating all together.

Despite the differences in dating backgrounds, I hear the same message echoed time and again:

"I'm wonderful – so why am I still single?"

"I don't need help with online dating. After all, who knows me better than I do?"

"I'll just be myself, and then if they don't like me, that's just too bad for them."

"If I'm being myself, and putting my real self out there, how can I go wrong?"

"What could I need help with? Slapping a profile together isn't rocket science."

"I get tons of emails from my online dating profile, so it must be great, right?"

Online dating *seems* simple, but those who have tried it and have just ended up older, with smaller bank accounts, but still single, know that while the certain aspects of dating can be easy, the *finding love* with online dating aspect can be hard. If it were as easy as slapping up a couple pictures and a brief self-description and meeting Your Match the next day, everyone who wanted to be would be married by now!

If you heard your own voice above, you – like my clients – are right that being yourself is critically important. But you may be missing the larger picture. You not only have to be yourself, you have to present yourself – *market* yourself – in such a way, and in such a place, that Your Match can find you.

In order to WOW someone with your amazing personality, you have to get in front of him or her first!

21

That's where services like Meet Your Match Online come in. We bridge the gap between signing up for an online dating service and sitting back with fingers crossed and actually finding *success* with online dating. If you've been dating for a while and you keep finding exactly the wrong people, it doesn't necessarily mean there's something wrong with you, but there IS something wrong with your *methods*.

It might be your profile, your photos, or the site you're on that's holding you back. Or, if you don't know who you're actually looking for, it could be *you* holding yourself back. After all, if you don't know what you want, you certainly have a much lower chance of finding it.

What I've discovered in reviewing thousands of online dating profiles that many online daters don't realize is that a lot of what makes them so amazing – what makes them stand out in "real life" – is lost because of the medium in which they are communicating. The dry wit and sarcasm that is so charming in person can come across as just plain mean in an email. That chatty and outgoing nature that sets others at ease in person can come across as boring and long-winded in your four-page email.

Knowing how to date online the *right way* increases your chances of attracting the right person and ensuring that you'll get a chance to meet in person and let your date get to know the *real you*!

Regardless of how great you are, no matter how smart, or how witty of a writer, I guaranty you are making some of the mistakes I'll identify in this book. How am I so sure? Because it's nearly impossible to be impartial enough about your essay section or your photos to avoid making at least some of these mistakes. But don't worry – we're going to fix them!

Chapter 2: Overcoming Your Fear of "The Stigma"

"**H**ow did you meet?" He asks, smiling happily at the two of you. You look at each other for approval. *Can we tell him? What will he think?* He's your date's friend, so you give the nod of approval. "We met online." *Yep. There it is. That familiar grimace, quickly covered by the open-mouthed "Oh, I'm so happy for you," look of surprise and the forced gradual relaxation of the eyebrows as he works to come up with something inoffensive to say.* "Ohhhhh. Okay. I guess that's pretty common now?"

*   *   *

If you've been dating online for long, you've probably had this exact scenario play out more times than you care to recall. You can't really blame people for being curious, and that's really all it is - curiosity. A decade ago there was practically no such thing as online dating (at least not as we know it today). Although almost everyone knows someone whose relationship started online, there aren't a lot of people out there who openly discuss it. The resulting whispers and intrigue are to be expected, but that doesn't necessarily make answering these types of questions any easier for couples who met online.

Five years ago the answer to the infamous "shall we tell people we met online" question would have been a resounding "No!" followed by an agreement to say that you met at the place where you had your first date. (How very sneaky and clever of you.) Some of the men I dated wanted to use this tactic, though I never agreed. I only stayed in relationships so long as I thought there was a future, and didn't want a future built on a lie we'd have to tell a thousand times over if things worked out.

> *In addition to the "Are we dating exclusively?" conversation, modern dating has now grown to include the "Are we telling people we met online?" conversation.*

In the past few years, so many people have joined online dating communities, and so many marriages have resulted from online dating matches, that The Stigma is slowly subsiding. More and more of us are finally coming out and letting people know, with as little self-consciousness as we can muster, that, "Yes, we met online. So... how 'bout that rainstorm we had last week, huh?"

Origin of The Stigma:
The Dawn of Online Dating

Just ten years ago, "meeting online" often signified an exchange of sexually-suggestive emails from the darkness of your den or dorm room with some anonymous screen name in a super-sketchy chat room, exchanging too much personal information, receiving a picture of a model (or genitalia), and meeting your pen pal at some private location (i.e. being lured to your doom). If you lived to tell the tale, it would usually begin with a story of the massive amounts of deception on the part of the person you met (including fake pictures, fake background stories, and fake names), and conclude with a harrowing tale of your near-demise and skin-of-your-teeth escape.

Nearly a decade ago, a gal I know had just such an experience. She went to meet a gentleman in person with whom she had been corresponding for some time. She arrived (a bit early) at the designated meeting point. She waited for quite a while and when he did not show up she drove across the street to get some gas for her car. He quickly approached her there (we can only assume he had been watching her the whole time) and demanded to know why she was so late. In addition to his rude and frightening approach, this woman was also put off by the fact that the man looked *nothing* like his picture (not the same height, age, or race – not the same person at all!).

He demanded that she follow him (she in her car and he in his) to a secondary, undisclosed location in a more remote area. She was so shaken by the whole event that she initially followed him, not knowing what else to do, but when she realized she was safe in her car, she tried to elude him by pulling a U-turn. He then flipped a U too and began to follow her. Driving in an unfamiliar neighborhood, she became disoriented and took a turn down a dead end road. He pulled his car across the road, got out, and approached her car on foot. She was trapped. Thanks to some panic-induced stunt man driving on her part (on the sidewalk and over a few lawns) she managed to escape him, and survive to tell the tale.

She and I (and now you) can learn some important lessons from that terrifying experience, including the importance of *sharing* what can go wrong with others to keep them safe too.

The Stigma: Where Are We Now?

We have come a long way since these dark days. Services such as Match.com (with a purported 96 Million registered users) and eHarmony (37 Million registered users)[3] have brought online dating into the sanitizing light of day and onto the public stage. These companies help organize the clumsy, and potentially dangerous, world of meeting strangers online. Because you must pay for many of their services, they do provide some measure of weeding out those who are just there to mess with people or run scams, but aren't willing to invest $30+ per month to do that (especially because that requires using a credit card and leaving a paper trail).

Some daters still fear running across a friend, family member, or co-worker online.

Despite the growing legitimacy of online dating, many are still hesitant or embarrassed to tell even their closest friends they are dating online. A secret fear I hear from many of the online daters I've talked with is that someone they know might stumble across their profile. Or worse, that a dating service will match them with a

[3] http://www.confirio.com/blog/?p=19. Retrieved March 29, 2011.

friend, colleague, or co-worker. In fact, a client of mine actually had this happen:

I'd been corresponding with Dave[4] for about a week on a free online dating website. He was cute, funny, and we had a lot in common – we both loved soccer and international travel. We exchanged numbers and decided to meet at a soccer bar in Seattle in order to watch an English Premier League match. He walked in, gave me a smile, and put me right at ease.

After ordering breakfast, we started talking about where we grew up. I grew up in Seattle, and he in one of the suburbs. He asked me where I went to high school, and my response nearly made him spit out his coffee.

"Riverview," I said. Mindful of the reputation our high school had of producing people of privilege, I started babbling on about how I wasn't like the "typical" Riverview graduate. Meaning that I didn't have a silver spoon in my mouth.

He turned bright red, and managed to stammer out "Riverview. Uh, funny. I graduated from there two years before you did."

Turns out that we'd gone to the same small, private high school, and didn't recognize each other on the website! We weren't friends there, just acquaintances, but I always thought he was super nice.

After an awkward five minutes, I exclaimed, "Small world!" and we turned back to watching soccer and talking about the game. We ended up having a pret-

[4] Names of people and schools are changed to protect the innocent.

ty good time, but it felt like I was hanging out with a sports buddy rather than with a potential romantic partner. The date ended with a hug, and a "that was fun." But that was our last outing together.

Even though this dater found herself in a potentially awkward situation, she was able to make the best of it, laugh at the absurdity of going out with someone you know – and not realizing you know them – and keep after her goal. I'm happy to report that she is now in a great relationship with a man who did *not* go to her high school (or to her college or grad school), who she met online.

The bottom line is that most singles have used or will use online dating services at one time or another. There aren't that many *great* services either, so chances are you will come across someone you know (or several someones) and that they'll come across you. What's great is that sometimes seeing someone in a different light (such as the way they portray themselves online) can help you to find a new connection from a past friendship!

Nowadays, everyone knows someone who is dating online, and many people you know who are dating or married met online. Online daters are becoming the majority and, as such, should prepare to shake loose The Stigma, and loudly and proudly answer the question, "How did you meet?" with "We met online!"

Chapter 3:
Avoiding Online
Dating Burn Out

M any are prompted to sign up for online dating
when another relationship comes to an end,
when overcome by the frustration of not finding
anyone when looking in the "real world" (I always cringe
when I hear it phrased like that), or when attempting to
avoid less elegant alternatives like trolling the bar scene,
unsuccessfully searching for Mr. or Miss Right (who
would be far too decent to be found at a bar at that un-
godly hour anyway).

Although many are initially leery of online dating,
once the screening tests have been taken and the profile
is prepared, the experience can be exciting and fun. As
you browse (depending on your subscription and service)
the list of potential dates available to you, you will – I
hope – begin to feel empowered and excited at the possi-
bilities. Some compare it to shopping online; you browse
through your options and select the traits you're looking

for – order love online with just one easy click. If you don't keep your feet, the sea of potential suitors that opens up when one enters the online world can swallow you right up.

The first couple days online can be an exciting rush. Each day you come home to see who might have written; you check your email to see whether she "winked" back at you or whether he "nudged" you. You scan emails coming in from those who the mighty Internet's supercomputers

> *Some have compared the feeling of online dating to online shopping; you see what's available, and select what you want – order love online with just one easy click.*

have judged to be compatible with you. Getting lots of winks, emails, or other contact from fine looking gentlemen or ladies is a wonderful ego boost. Sadly, though, the ecstasy of online dating is often short-lived; the subsequent fall can be quick and the landing hard.

The Wake-Up Call: Don't Burn Out!

My business' research indicates that the primary reason people give up on online (or all!) dating is due to feelings of disappointment and frustration. Somehow, we have found a million ways to disappoint each other through online dating, often before we even meet. Over the years I've heard countless tales of frustration and disappointment, including the following: [5]

---

[5] Whenever quoting or summarizing our clients or respondents I have changed names to protect anonymity.

Adrianne: *When I showed up for the date, I felt like I was meeting his older, heavier broth-er. His profile picture must have been at least eight years old, and he clearly lied about his age too. I would have gone out with the real him, since it was primarily his personality and hobbies I was attracted to. But I won't see him again. I just can't get past the lies.*

Martin: *I winked, I emailed, I saved her as a favorite, and I sent her an instant message. She never responded. Can't she even let me know she's not interested?*

Denise: *We emailed back and forth for weeks. As soon as I sent him my phone number, it was like he disappeared from the face of the planet. How is wanting a phone call coming on too strong?*

Julie: *Every single guy that writes to me seems to only be interested in me because I'm Asian. I'm so creeped out. How do I find someone who can see past my race?*

Adam: *Before we met, we'd talk on the phone and text for hours. After our first date, she told me she just wasn't feeling it. But we got along so well; how could that be?*

Becca: *We have so much in common, but he won't write back to me. Can't he see how per-fect we would be for each other?*

These responses are just a sampling of the com-plaints I've heard, and to be fair they are justified. Just like in real life, people can be rude, cruel, deceitful, and mean online. However, daters can also read too much into each others' behavior. Knowing how to see the warning signs can help, but some amount of disappointment and hurt is inevitable. The key is to not take it too personally, and to never let it get between you and finding Your Match.

Think of it this way: if someone is a jerk to you, they are just doing a great job of helping to let you know that they are NOT the one you're looking for!

I will provide you with as much advice as possible to avoid the most common pitfalls, but I will also ask that, as much as possible, you be kind to each other out there in the online dating world. There's a quote of unknown origin, "Sometimes you're the pigeon, and sometimes you're the statue." My *goal* is that after reading this book, you will be able to avoid being the statue as much as possible. My *request* is that you do your best to avoid being the pigeon too.

Chapter 4:
The Number One
Reason Daters Fail

I have a great friend who I've known for decades. She is one of those "live life to the fullest" types that I often envy. Her dating strategy is the same as her life strategy – she dives into every situation head-first, throwing caution to the wind. She'll be the first to admit that this has occasionally resulted in her getting badly hurt, but as soon as she recovers, she somehow manages to get right back into the game, and prepare herself for her next dive.

I have heard her say more than once, "You know, Laura, I think this one is The One!!" Although she has been wrong (and let's face it, who among us hasn't?!), I am more confident that she will find Her Match than I am about many other singles I meet simply because of her unwavering faith that Her Match is out there. I too believe that he is out there for her, so I know that she *will* find him.

Despite her spirit, at certain points – perhaps after a particularly heinous date – I'm sure she questions (and I know you and I have asked ourselves), "Is this really worth it?" Is it worth the time, money, stress, and heartache for the chance to find My Match? She has firmly decided that it is. But not everyone may agree, which leads to the number one reason that daters will fail:

THEY DON'T *WANT* TO BE SUCCESSFUL.

They aren't looking for – or ready for – a long-term, committed relationship with another person. The result is they either won't find it, or will sabotage something great if they do!

Sure, people fail for many other reasons: they give up too fast, they are unwilling to go outside their comfort zones, they have personal issues that prevent them from becoming close to another person... the list goes on. But above all other reasons, daters fail because of self-sabotage. It is *perfectly fine* to be single. There's nothing wrong with being single! If you're not ready to be in a committed relationship, more power to you for staying single until you are. The timing cannot be forced.

For most of you reading this book, though, there comes a time in your life when you *are* ready. At that time, you can feel it in your heart and down to your bones. You know in your soul that you are ready for someone to cuddle up with in front of the fireplace with and with whom to weather life's storms.

Use the questions below to think seriously about whether you are ready for a relationship. Don't tell your fellow online daters looking for serious relationships that you're ready for meaningful love if you're not. If you're on a journey to "find yourself" you will need to walk that path alone (that is, not with someone you're casually dating who is looking for more). Straighten out your own life first, and then come fully prepared and emotionally ready for a loving relationship.

Are You Ready For Love?

1. Do you still feel the need to "sew your wild oats," "play the field," or "browse the menu" for a while?

While it is true that women tend to be more focused on finding a husband than men are focused on finding a wife, both genders do need time to date around a bit. That doesn't mean they need to get into sexual relationships with everyone they meet, but there is value in dating different people to come to know one's own likes and dislikes. For some, it may be hard to determine what is truly important to them in another person until they have dated people that have some of those qualities. Similarly, it might be hard to know what you just can't stand until you've experienced that too.

However, there does come a time – some people describe it as a switch being flipped inside of them – where men and women become less interested in browsing and more interested in finding that one true love of their life. If you've gotten there and you've dated someone who isn't there yet (or, God-forbid, married someone who isn't there yet), you know what I mean!

Until that switch gets flipped, you won't have the kind of success I'm talking about with online dating. It might be fun for a while, especially if you're trying people out to see what works, but you won't be in a place to find Your Match.

However, if that switch *has* been flipped for you, and you're *done* being single and ready for something more in your life, something that feels more like *forever* than *for as long as it's fun*, participating in online dating services – especially paid sites – is absolutely worth your time.

If, after reading this book, you feel like you're unsure where you stand, or need a bit more one-on-one help, know that you don't have to go it alone. To get the most out of your time dating online, you can invest in a service like Meet Your Match Online to focus yourself and target your search. With the techniques you'll learn and steps we'll take together, you'll see –

> *Imagine not spending one more Thanksgiving answering questions about why you're still single...*

when you are ready – how you'll save *so much money* on online dating services by making them work FAST for you, so you may only have to date for months, not a few years. Imagine not spending one more Thanksgiving answering questions about why you haven't settled down yet...

2. Are you being honest with your intentions?

As we've discussed, there are plenty of sites out there for people who are just looking for a good time, and to get some dating experience. There is *nothing wrong with that*! Certain free sites let you make a note of your intentions so that other daters can see exactly what you're looking for. Use those services to be up-front and clear about your expectations. You will attract like-minded people and have an experience of the type you are seeking.

That said, if you are not looking to find long-lasting, loving relationships, don't waste the time or break the hearts of those who are. Stay away from the "serious relationships" sites like eHarmony – and avoid paying those high monthly rates – until you know it's time to find Your Match. Most of all, don't mislead others by stating that you're looking for something long-term if you're not. As with all other areas of your profile, BE HONEST.

3. Are you generally happy with yourself?

If you are unhappy with your lot in life, if you don't love who you are as a person, or if you cannot be happy by yourself, then you will not be successful in finding Your Match.

Being ready to accept someone else's love into your life requires a certain amount of self-acceptance. Some of this comes with age, some comes with life experience, and some comes with help from others. If you need help, ask for it. Don't waste anymore of your own time repeating the same mistakes and wondering why things aren't working out.

If you feel you're a little rough around the edges, have some "emotional baggage," or notice that you keep repeating bad dating choices, you may benefit from a couple of coun-

Don't blow your chance with the right person because you didn't have your life together.

37

seling sessions. Think how much easier it will be to attract a well-balanced person, if you're feeling your best, too.[6]

You don't want to meet Your Match until you are ready to bring her or him the best version of you that you can. Don't blow your chance with the right person because you didn't have your life together.

Here are two emails a man who was registered at an online dating site sent, unsolicited, to a lovely woman whose profile he viewed and apparently found not to his liking. This is an example of someone clearly not ready to be dating. This is an exact quote – grammar and spellings errors are his own:

> *"[Subject Line: You're so immature] "I'm pretty sure you've had "friends" matching your description of an ideal guy. Do yourself a favour and stop fooling yourself. I hate girls like you, such hipocrits. Also, religion is the worst thing that ever happened to human kind, no one with some brains believes in all that crap."*

Although the woman did not reply or otherwise engage with him, he followed up a month later with this email:

> *"Hey I just wanted to apologize for being a complete ass, I was in really bad shape when I wrote my first e-mail... pretty hurt and angry at life, I was losing my mid... I feel really stupid. You're a real catch so I hope you find what you're looking for."*

---

[6] Note: If you do want to talk to someone, check with your insurance – often they will pay for some or all of the cost of counseling.

So please, learn from this! Get any help you might need before you get online. *Don't be this guy.*

Find Your Motivation

The work you will need to do to be successful may be challenging, and burn out is possible. If you have determined that you *are* ready for love, ask yourself how you know. What feelings are motivating you to find Your Match – your *forever* love? When you can answer these questions, you've found your motivation.

Hold onto that as you look. My methods *will* work for you, but they may take some time... especially if Your Match is currently in another relationship, in another state, or otherwise unavailable. Not everyone will be as lucky as My Match, who only used online dating for three months before he met His Match (before I found him, that is).

> *To be successful be single, be visible, and be emotionally available!*

While so much of dating success is out of your control, there are certain things you can focus on doing proactively so you'll have success when you meet Your Match: (1) be single – if you're in a relationship with no future, get out of it ASAP; (2) be visible – market yourself in places where Your Match is likely to be looking for you; and (3) be emotionally available when you finally meet. If you have issues with an ex, deal with them now. Don't wait until you're with someone great to let all that damage come flooding out and drown the other person.

When deciding whether to continue (or start fresh) with online dating, review the three questions in this chapter. Make sure you're ready to date, and dating for the right reasons. If you're not ready, you're wasting your money and your time (and someone else's time) – time that would be better spent trying to figure out what you want in life or working through barriers standing in the way of your happiness. If you find yourself in that situation, consider taking your profile down and doing some work on yourself before getting back into dating. You'll be doing the right thing, and will be putting yourself on the path to finding love that much faster.

If you're dating (or getting ready to date) for the right reasons, check in with yourself about whether you are committed to putting in the time and effort necessary to make the use of an online dating service subscription worth your while. If you feel like you're wasting money because you're not spending the time it takes, try switching over to a free service for a few months and until you determine that you're ready for something serious.

Finally, if you start feeling discouraged, before giving in to the feelings of disappointment remember your motivation. Remember the hope you had when you first signed up, the hope you get before every new first date. Cling to that hope and kindle it when you can.

Setting Goals

If you find the process generally overwhelming, try setting some reasonable goals for yourself and write them down. For example, agree that you will make some form of contact (e.g. a wink on Match.com) with at least three people per week, and will send or respond to an email at least once per week. Agree to go on at least one date per month (unless it would just be leading someone on, which is strictly forbidden in my world of dating rules).

My friend, a lovely lady who works in real estate, says her father taught her to ALWAYS say yes when a new guy asked her out on a date. Although I wouldn't recommend that for my clients (it would result in too much wasted time with people they know they would *never* end up with), it was certainly a good way for her to meet new people and learn more about them and herself. And it did work for her – she found Her Match in college and was married by age 25.[7]

When deciding whether to go on a date, keep in mind that you need to give people the chance to impress you *in person*. Even if it doesn't end up in a true romance, you're still giving yourself the experience of getting to know someone new. They don't need to be obvious husband or wife material – strangers rarely are! Just look for commonalities and someone who you think would make a great friend. A lot of the process is simply about going outside your comfort zone.

Take a moment to think about a realistic goal you can set – right now, today! Use the space that follows to write it down and to commit yourself to it:

My Goals:

_____

_____

_____

_____

_____.

_____

[7] It would certainly make life easier for guys if more women start to develop this philosophy, though! Imagine no possibility of rejection! That certain someone you've had your eye on might not be as unattainable as you think!

Sort Your Way to Success

I was once told, "You don't have to be good at finding the right person, you just have to be good at sorting out the ones who are wrong." This advice fundamentally changed the way I dated (in an epically good way). I realized the one mistake I was making in every bad relationship – staying in it too long!

I stayed in bad relationships months after I knew they would never work. It's humiliating to admit, because I hate what it says about me and where my confidence level was back in my dating days, but I took men back even after they disclosed they had cheated on me!

I look back now and wonder what I could have been thinking, but I realize that at the time I was focused on "making it work" or "getting through it together." For each terrible match I dated I always thought, "Oh, he has so much potential," and took him back. Now I would say, "He's a loser, and I'm lucky he's making it so obvious." Get rid of him - fast!

While my day-to-day routine limited the number of people I could meet offline, my profile was available to millions of potential suitors online.

Learn from my mistakes. Stick with the goals you just set for yourself. Give people a chance, but if you *know* they are not right, it's time to move on. Don't miss the right one because you're too busy clinging to a relationship that will never be fulfilling in the ways you deserve.

Patience will also play a role. Not everyone will find his or her Match on the first pass. It took me around 15 bad first dates (and some that led to bad relationships too) to find My Match. In contrast, I was the first person My Match ever met online. Keep in mind we're talking 10 – 20 dates here, not hundreds!

This *is doable*, but you may have to try a variety of methods, and you *will* have to get outside of your comfort zone. I would never have found the love of my life spending all my time sitting in the law library (we confirmed that he – living 60 miles away – would not have likely stumbled across me in the school's library). Nor would I have found him in my law office, at the marketing events I attended for work, at the various church groups I joined in my neighborhood, on my summer softball team, at my drop-in winter volleyball league, or through the volunteer organizations in which I participated. Why? Because he wasn't there! Nor was he "almost" at any of those places. Indeed, without online dating, it is highly unlikely our paths would ever have crossed.

> *Without online dating, My Match's path and mine would never have crossed.*

Being willing to take the risk and face disappointment through online dating is no small challenge, but the reward far outweighs these risks. Maybe Your Match is online right now. Don't make him or her wait any longer for you!

Chapter 5:
Precautions for
(Online) Dating

Done correctly, online dating can be fun and extremely rewarding. Done incorrectly, online dating has cost some people their life savings and others their *lives*. The information in this chapter may save both, so pay attention and use this information going forward.

With online dating, as with offline dating, there are certain precautions you *must* take to protect yourself, whether you are a man or a woman. Although the large majority of people are truly out there looking for a compatible match, there are also those who roam the internet (and bars, clubs, etc.) looking to prey on the unsuspecting. Many who read this information think, "This is so obviously a scam! I would never fall for this!" But there are thousands who do, and as long as that is the case, I will continue to share this information so that readers know how to prepare themselves and how to stay safe.

Common Scams

As the sophistication of online dating services has grown over the years, so has the sophistication of those preying on online daters. Please review the following scams carefully to familiarize yourself with how scammers are (very successfully) defrauding online daters, often unburdening them of hundreds of thousands of dollars.

The Re-Shipping Scam. The objective of re-shipping scams is to ship something from person A to person B. Person A doesn't want to ship directly because the goods are stolen or were purchased with fraudulent credit card information. So instead, they use a patsy – a middleman – an online dater. They use online dating services or chat rooms to find their unwitting accomplice under the guise of friendship or love.

The shipper (person A) will either befriend someone they meet online through a social networking site or chatroom or begin a romantic long-distance relationship with an online dater. Often times they will send a small gift as a token of their love and affection (and as a way to get your home address). Soon, an "emergency" will arise that will require you to receive a package on their behalf and ship it on to someone else (person B) who will almost always be in another country. Once you allow this to happen, the floodgates will open and the packages will keep coming until you are contacted by the defrauded merchants, until you wise up to the scam, or until the police arrive at your doorstep to arrest you – whichever comes first.

The Mail Order Bride Scam. Whereas the re-shipping scam is more frequently perpetrated on women (whose instinct it is to help another in a time of need), the mail order bride scams are targeted toward men. In these scams, young, beautiful, foreign women will form a fast relationship with American men, "falling in love" with them very quickly. As soon as the groundwork is laid, the women will ask the men to help them come to the United States so they can be together. The women will say they have found a group that can help with the visas and putting all the paperwork together, but the men will have to pay for this service because the women are short on funds.

After the man pays, arrangements are made for the woman to come to the United States. Invariably, however, there will be some last minute emergency that will stop them from making it and require some additional influx of cash. Whether or not the man pays it, the woman will never arrive. Remember, men, if she's thirty years younger than you and somehow it just seems too good to be true, it probably IS!

The Business Man Scam. This scam is generally perpetrated against the "mature dater" set, and usually against women. In this fraud, the scammer will develop a relationship with (usually) a senior citizen and position himself as a successful business man. After building the relationship, the business man will present the dater with a fabulous investment opportunity. After he obtains the dater's financial information and passwords, or even the investment itself, he will disappear with her life savings or entire retirement account.

> *He will tell you that he loves you, and then make off with your life savings.*

A common twist on this scam is where the business man will pose as a tax consultant or advisor. He will use this title to obtain the woman's financial information and, as before, make off with her life savings.

The Military Man Scam. In this fraudulent scheme, a woman will form a relationship with a person pretending to be a United States serviceman serving overseas.[8] The two will correspond regularly, but never meet. He will tell her quickly that he is falling in love, and that is when the problems start. As in the mail order bride scam, the man will start to have many issues with which it seems his new love is the only one that can help. Resolution of the problems always seems to involve wiring funds.

As straightforward and obvious as these schemes may all sound, people are losing millions of dollars to scammers. Women in the United States have been reported to have lost over $200,000 *per scam*, and one woman from the United Kingdom lost over $400,000 in one military man scam. Heed the following warnings to make sure you'll stay safe from these fraudulent schemes and spot a scammer who might be coming after you.

Avoid Becoming A Victim Of Fraud

Do not make the mistake of sharing too much personal information – especially right away. This not only includes big ticket items like your social security number, passwords, address, credit card number, and names of your banking institutions, but also small things, like your exact date of birth.

---

[8] I want to highlight that these are *international criminals* pulling the scams, *not actual U.S. military men and women* defrauding online daters. There are many men and women who are presently abroad and using U.S. online dating services, hoping to form relationships with people they can meet in person upon their return to the U.S. or chat with via Skype until they return.

It is natural for someone you're meeting (or newly dating) to want to know some amount of personal information about you, but pay special attention if it seems too soon, or if they get angry if (1) you say no to a request for information; (2) you ask why they want the information; or (3) you convey your concerns about disclosing certain information. Use the following Scammer Checklist anytime you think things are starting to smell fishy.

Although any one of these items may not indicate a scam, if you start to see several with one person, think twice (or more, if necessary) about responding:

SCAMMER CHECKLIST

☐ Have you been on a dating or social networking site in the past 6 months? If so, have you started a correspondence with someone from it?

☐ Does the person with whom you're corresponding seem to be in a big hurry to get your information to email or chat outside the confines of the dating service?[9]

☐ Does the person's profile vanish from the dating service, but then he or she reappears and contacts you from a different user name?[10]

☐ Does the person claim to be recently widowed, or generate another story that tugs at the heartstrings?

☐ Does the person ask for your address under the guise of sending flowers or gifts (think re-shipping scam!)?

---

[9] Many scammers will try to communicate with you outside of the anonymity of the dating service quickly. They may be "working" hundreds of different daters at a time, and if they are flagged, their profiles will be taken down. They want to get your personal information as quickly as possible to ensure the scam can continue even if their profile is removed.

[10] When the scammers *are* flagged and their profiles removed, they will start up again with a new profile, often on the same site. If they haven't gotten you off the service yet, they will contact you again with their new profile in an attempt to continue the scam on you.

- ☐ Does the person make an unusually high number of grammar and/or spelling errors (so many that you begin to think they may not speak English)?

- ☐ Does the person talk about destiny or fate? Does it seem they are driving the relationship very quickly toward love?

- ☐ Does the person claim to be from the United States but is currently working, living, or traveling abroad?

- ☐ Does the person make plans to visit you but have a last minute emergency that prevents them from following through?

- ☐ Does the person ask you for money or to cash a check? (This is perhaps THE BIGGEST red flag!)

When someone you barely know asks you for huge favors or makes it seem as though you are their only hope, ask yourself why this person has *no other* close family, friend, or even business associate to whom he or she can turn instead of a complete stranger (you!) who he or she just met online. Don't let the anonymity of the internet fool you; consider whether his or her requests would make sense to you if you were meeting face to face. Keep this checklist handy!

Avoid Becoming a Victim of Assault[11]

Although the majority of these tips to avoid becoming the victim assault are directed toward women, there is important information here for men, too. Men should read this section to have a better understanding of why a woman may respond to your advances in an unexpected way. For example, if you are trying to be chivalrous by picking her up from her home from the date, *good for you*! I – and many other women out there

---

[11] For more on this topic, I highly recommend (especially to women) reading Gavin de Becker's book, "The Gift of Fear."

– love chivalry! But understand that she may turn your offer down, preferring to keep her address and other information private for a while. Don't take it as her being a "man-hater" – just respect what she's doing to watch out for her personal safety.

Above everything else, the number one safety tip to remember is *trust your instincts and act with caution.* Staying vigilant can save your life.

Personal safety expert Gavin de Becker has identified pre-incident indicators ("PINS"). Heeding these warnings and listening to your instincts that tell you something isn't right can save your life. De Becker lists the following PINS to watch for, many of which can be identified as early as in the first email:

> *Trust your instincts and act with caution. Staying vigilant can save your life.*

- o **Forced Teaming**. This occurs when a person tries to pretend that he or she has something in common with you or that he or she is in the same predicament as you when that isn't really true.

- o **Charm and Niceness**. People often are disarmed by a nice smile, clean cut appearance, or friendly demeanor. However, where predators are concerned, this is a tool in the arsenal; they are being polite and friendly in order to manipulate another's behavior.

- o **Too Many Details**. If a person is lying he will add excessive details because he believes it makes him sound more credible.

- o **Typecasting**. A predator may try to lob an insult at you or "typecast" you in a certain role (e.g. the rude neighbor, the stuck up girl) to get you to talk to him when you would otherwise ignore him.

○ **Loan Sharking**. Giving unsolicited help and expecting favors in return (e.g. helping you to carry something when you didn't ask for help).

○ **The Unsolicited Promise**. This is a promise to do (or not do) something when no such promise is requested. The unsolicited promise is almost always broken. For example, an unsolicited, "I promise I'll leave you alone after this," usually means you will not be left alone. Similarly, an unsolicited "I promise I won't hurt you" usually means the person *intends* to hurt you.

○ **Discounting the Word "No."** There's a reason salespeople won't take "no" for an answer. Refusing to accept rejection is a tried and true way for people to talk you into doing something that makes you uncomfortable or suspicious.

Depending on the motive of the helper, the exact same action can feel completely different when done by someone with good intentions or done by someone with bad intentions.

For example, imagine two scenarios – in both, you have spilled your groceries on your way up the stairs to your walk-up apartment and someone comes to help you pick them up. In the first scenario, the person scoops them up and helps you put them back into your bag; you thank him, and he continues on his way. You think, "How nice!" and continue up the stairs.

In the second scenario, the person comments on how flimsy bags these days are, and that they rip apart on him all the time too (*forced teaming*). As he helps put the groceries back in your bag, he flashes you a smile and grazes your arm (*charm and niceness*). Then he offers to help you get the bags the rest of the way to your apartment, an offer that you decline. He insists (*discounting the word no*), and promises he'll let you get on with your day after that (*unsolicited promise*).

After all this, alarm bells should be going off in your head to not let this person get within ten feet of you. Always err on the side of caution in these scenarios, even if it means you must be rude. (Remember, if the other person were being respectful of you, you would not have to be rude.) Insist you will carry on without him, forcefully if necessary. Your safety comes first.

Especially For Women: Staying Safe On A First Date

Before you start your online dating journey you will need to set an online dating "protocol" for yourself. Follow this protocol *every time* - regardless of how you met, how sweet the guy seems, or how perfect he appears to be for you. Just because you met someone through a friend of a friend, and not online, doesn't make him or her inherently safe. Use the listed protocols for a *base level* of security, but please consider what other items you may want to add:

o **Take your time to send emails back and forth**. Develop a comfort level before you even give out your full name, and especially before giving another user your phone number. If the person is pushing to meet too quickly, such as the same day/night they wrote to you, that's a warning sign. If he or she is interested in a long-term relationship, then he or she can wait a week before getting to meet you in person.

o **Always talk on the phone before meeting**. You can learn a lot about a person through a phone conversation. It's a lot harder to fake a phone call than it is to fake a text message or an email, or to get someone to write it for you. When you talk on the phone, refer to the person's profile, and refer to email conversations you've had. Make sure you're speaking with the same person with whom you've been corresponding. If the person makes you feel uncomfortable on the phone, I guarantee it will be worse in person. Thank him for his time, and let him know you're just not feeling a spark. If he continues to call, ask him not to call anymore. Block his number if necessary.

- **Always meet in public**. And after you meet in a public place, *stay* in a public place. Predators often use the strategy of providing a public place to meet and then applying pressure once you've met in person to go to a more secluded location. Decline the offer to go somewhere private. If he persists, end the date immediately.

- **As a corollary to the previous rule, never meet in a private location.** This is important enough to bear repeating: *Never meet in a private location* for your first date, even if he or she tells you that the plan is to go somewhere public after that. A great idea for a first date is meeting mid-morning at a heavily trafficked coffee shop. This will give you enough time to get a good sense of the person, and an easy escape if it's a nightmare. If he or she is unwilling to meet during the day (but be conscientious that it's not during his or her

> *NEVER meet in a private location for your first date, even if the plan is to go somewhere public after that.*

workday) or in a public place, and doesn't have a good reason why, it's a big red flag.

o **Stay in Control.** It is extremely important to keep your wits about you on a first (and second, and third...) date. Stay sober and stay in control of your situation. Drive yourself to the date, don't do anything to impair your judgment, keep an eye on your drink at all times, and drive yourself home. (If your drink is out of your sight, which can happen if you use the restroom, if you're at a restaurant don't hesitate to ask the waitstaff for a new glass. You can tell your server that there's something floating around in it.) If you don't have a car, take a taxi or bus. Don't leave your safety in the hands of a stranger.

o **Use the buddy system.** Remember the trick from elementary school? It still works. Every time you go to meet someone, let a buddy know. Give your buddy as much information as you have about the person: screen name, phone number, first and last name, how you met (e.g. through which service), and a physical description. Tell him or her where you are going and when you plan to be back. Tell your buddy you will call when you get back. Then, CALL when you get back. Give him or her a time when they should check with you if they haven't yet heard from you. You can even mention to your date, "I told my friend Sarah I was going out with you, Mr. 'NWMountainMan,' today so she's looking forward to a report when I get back!"

> *If you don't feel safe, don't worry about being rude. Say goodbye and leave.*

55

These tips are an excellent starting place, but always trust your instincts. If you're sensing danger or trouble *heed these feelings*. You may not know why you're getting a bad vibe from someone, but listen to your internal alarm system nonetheless. While dating online should be fun and ideally yield a lasting, loving, trust-filled relationship, there are many ways to go very wrong.

Be careful and have fun!

PART TWO: THE KEYS TO SUCCESS

The most important things you will need to do to find love are: (1) avoid dating the wrong types, (2) start with a clean slate (i.e. don't repeat old bad habits or stay in bad relationships), (3) identify who you're looking for, and (4) get yourself in front of an audience in which such a person is likely to be found.

Chapter 6:
What's Your Type?

Based on our childhoods and past personal experiences, we're all drawn to different types of people. In the process that will unfold in Part Two, you will begin to learn about your previous patterns and who will be a better match for you. Before you begin to work through the steps of this process, let's explore some "types" that you may be attracted to but who will end up being a waste of your time rather than Your Match.

What's Your Type?

Mr. Almost Right/Miss Close Enough. Perhaps the MOST dangerous of all of the "types" is the one who is *almost* but not quite right. Dating such a person often results in years of dating ending in a devastating breakup and the feeling that you've wasted your best years with the wrong person. In a close-but-no-cigar relationship, often *both* people in the couple know that the other is not their Match. However, they will continue dating each other because (1) they are both conflict avoidant; (2) both are scared to be alone or to have to go back out into the dating world; (3) the relationship began when the couple was young and they are unaware of how much better things could be; (4) their lives – living together, friendship groups – have become so intertwined that they cannot easily separate; or (5) a combination of these reasons.

> *Even if someone is great, you should still break up if he or she is not great FOR YOU!*

Regardless of the reasons for staying together, this is the hardest relationship to end – far worse than ending a bad relationship. Often times, these relationships will have a lot of bad behavior lurking under the surface too; passive-aggressive hostility is usually rampant, as each person may passively try to get the other to break up with him or her by treating him or her poorly to force distance between them. Without an obvious reason to break up, the couple takes the path of least resistance and stays together. But there *is an incredibly important reason to break up!* You DESERVE an amazing relationship with someone who would move the sun and the moon to be with you. If you're not in it, you MUST move on.

The Serial Dater. The Serial Dater may be equally common among men as among women. These folks are the ones who seem never to be alone, but rather are always half of a couple. Such daters may spend years in each relationship, or simply hop from one significant other to the next with only a few months spent with each one. After a breakup, they say things like, "I think I'll take a few months off from dating," or "This time, I think I'll be single for a while to just take some time out for me." Invariably, though, they'll have a boyfriend or girlfriend again within the next two weeks.

Is this sounding familiar? A good test is to create a timeline from the time you started dating to the present. Subtract anytime in which you were married or engaged. From the time that is left over, how much of that time were you in relationships? How much of that time were you single? If you were in relationships 50% of your non-married life or less, you're probably safe. If you have been in various relationships 50% to 75% of the time, you're at risk for being a Serial Dater. If you've been in various relationships more than 75% of the time, chances are you *are* a Serial Dater. If so, think about why you haven't been alone? What feelings came up when you were dumped or after you dumped someone? What motivated you to get into another relationship?

The biggest concern with the Serial Dater is that he or she hasn't taken the time to find out who he or she is *alone* – to develop a sense of self-awareness or happiness without being part of a couple – a critical step to have taken in order to be a happy and healthy individual in a couple. Instead, such a person relies on the positive feel-feeling derived from being in a relationship to define him or herself. Watch out for Serial Daters to avoid being just another notch in a belt or crutch to prop someone up until he or she moves on. And, if you are a Serial Dater, take some serious time *alone* to explore the feelings that come up when you think about not being in a relationship. Make sure you are able to feel comfortable in your own skin before you launch into your next relationship.

> *One must have a sense of self-awareness and happiness without being part of a couple.*

Everybody's Favorite. I'm using this term as a euphemism for the person (male or female) who has been promiscuous. For men, this type is also known as a Player, and for women this type of women is also known by names too rude to print here. Although society tends to be harder on women with this reputation than men, both can be trouble. There's nothing that an "Everybody's Favorite" type can do to change his or her history or past choices, unfortunately, but the concern is less about the person's high numbers of sexual partners and more about *why* they have chosen to have so many partners. Such a person likely suffers from low self esteem (especially women in this category) and may struggle in a monogamous relationship with issues of fidelity (usually men).

If you choose to date this type of man or woman, make sure you take things slow. Get to know each other very well. Develop an understanding of the choices the person has made, and whether he or she has changed. If there were past self-esteem issues, have they since been resolved? How? If you're not careful in your selection with this type, you are likely to be used and disposed of quickly.

The Bad Boy/Girl. Whether we were drawn to him or her in our years of teenage rebellion, in a time of vulnerability after a breakup, or for reasons unknown, there just seems to be a universal appeal to the bad boys and bad girls. Is it the allure of danger? Our desire for the forbidden? There's a reason why the bad boys and bad girls never seem to have any trouble getting dates – and it's not because of their sweet personalities or their potential to win parent-of-the-year awards someday.

While there may be a time and a place for dating the bad boys and girls of the world, the time and place is *not* when you're looking for a serious relationship. If you find yourself continually dating this type, ask yourself whether you truly are looking for a long-term commitment. Often times we go for the bad boys and bad girls because we subconsciously know there's no future; we're trying to leave ourselves an easy escape route. Unfortunately, however, we're still the ones who usually end up getting hurt.

> *The time and the place for dating the bad boys and girls of the world is not when you're looking for a serious relationship.*

The Commitment-Phobe. This type seems to be most prevalent in men. (In contrast, women are more likely to be commitment-focused; potentially pushing commitment after only a couple dates.) While there are very few women who consciously seek commitment-phobic men, the real mis-step is not dumping him when you realize you have one on your hands. Whether he doesn't want to be exclusive, doesn't want to use the word "boyfriend" after you are clearly in an exclusive relationship, is hesitant to introduce you to his friends, or won't propose after a reasonable amount of time, there are lots of signs along the way that he's just not that excited about a future with you.[12]

---

[12] I'm using the word "reasonable" to hedge my bets. What is "reasonable" depends largely on your age and unique situation. To put some really basic guidelines on it, if you're in your early 20s, several years is probably good to date to make sure your lives are headed in a similar direction. If you're over 30, generally a year or two is plenty of time before an engagement.

It's up to you to know the timetable that's right for you. When I figured out what I wanted, I was vocal about my plans with any boyfriend who lasted beyond a couple months. I said, "I'm not going to be dating you for years and years. If we don't believe that this is headed toward marriage in at least a year, I'm out." That helped the "window shoppers" move along quickly, and made the ones who were actually interested think seriously about a future in a reasonable amount of time. In retrospect, a year timeline was probably even longer than necessary, but for the men who were serious, it seemed reasonable and not terrifying.

Even if you don't have this discussion outright with your significant other, do take stock every few months. If you're not on the same page about where you want the relationship to go (i.e. that you are looking for marriage, rather than just continued casual dating) after six to twelve months, think seriously about moving on. Your time is precious and you can't afford to waste it with someone who doesn't see you in his or her future.

> *Your time is precious and you can't afford to waste it with someone who doesn't see you in his or her future.*

The Bird With The Broken Wing. I'll confess, before I met My Match, this had always been my type (though not consciously chosen). I believe I thought that if I could fix each guy's metaphoric broken wing (whether he came from a broken home, had parents who didn't seem to love him, had been verbally or physically abused, or suffered from mental illness) then I could earn his love. After all, he would *have* to love me because I had fixed him, right? Wrong...for *so* many reasons.

First and foremost, neither I nor you should have to *earn* anyone's love. I was caring, compassionate, and loyal to a fault, and I was deserving of love. Second, I'm not a licensed psychotherapist, and I wasn't exactly equipped to heal decades-old, festering childhood traumas in grown men. It wasn't my place anyway.

Putting yourself in a situation where you have to "fix" your partner creates a terrible relationship dynamic. He or she may begin to see you as the sole source of his or her happiness (which isn't healthy), and in turn he or she may begin to see you as the source of his or her *unhappiness* (which isn't fair).

We all have our share of baggage, of course, but here's the key: You have to ask yourself whether you are in love with someone *and* he or she happens to have some baggage, or whether you are in love with him or her *because* of the baggage. If it's the latter, it's time to let that person go and find professional help. It's time to realize that you *deserve love* from someone who is emotionally present and available to you, and who is capable of loving you.

> *Ask yourself whether you are in love with someone and he or she happens to have baggage, or whether you are in love with him or her because of the baggage.*

The Mooch. Does he still live with his parents? Does it seem like she's just clinging to you for your money? In order to have a healthy adult relationship, you need to have two healthy adults. That means two people who are capable of standing on their own two feet. There's going to be some amount of financial inequity in any relationship, which can set up a difficult dynamic, but we all need to feel loved for who we are and not for what's in our wallets.

The best way to judge whether someone is a mooch is not by his or her current situation but by his or her future plans. It's possible that someone living at home may have a plan only to be there for a short time – while saving money for one or two years to by his or her own place, or may be home for a summer between years at graduate school. Find out what the agreement is, what the plans are; find out if he or she cooks and shops, does his or her own laundry. There's a big difference between the thrifty, future-oriented person I describe and the "Failure To Launch" scenario!

Chapter 7:
Making A Clean
Slate

Now that you've prepared yourself and determined that you're ready to proceed, it's time to get started. In this chapter, we'll work to identify negative patterns into which you've fallen in the past and provide some guidance about how to avoid repeating those same mistakes in the future.

Remember how I said that finding Your Match would involve some work on your part? This is where that work begins. But don't worry – it's going to be fun!

Recognizing Patterns

Let's start with an exercise to help you recognize your habits – good and bad. You can use the instructions below to complete this, or visit Meet Your Match Online's bonus content page to download and print (for free!) a detailed form to complete.[13]

STEP ONE: Identifying Key Relationships

Write down the name of your parent who is the same gender that you would normally date (e.g. heterosexual men, write down your mother's name), and the names of (up to) five people you have dated. If you have dated more than five people, please choose the five with whom you have had the longest or most meaningful relationships. We will use these six people going forward with the following exercises.

1. (Mother/Father)_____

2. _____

3. _____

4. _____

5. _____

6. _____

STEP TWO: Identifying Positive Traits

For each of these people, write down the traits about the person that you like the most. Write down the qualities that make them uniquely who they are. (E.g. Nurturing, excellent listener, problem-solver, optimistic, etc.) For your parent, obviously you did not choose him

---

[13] Our online form will take you through this process step by step, provideng plenty of room for you to write.
http://www.meetyourmatchonline.com/how-to-meet-your-match-online-bonus-material/

or her, but pull some memories from your childhood, teenage years, and young adulthood that you observed and admired in your parent. For those people who you dated, pay special attention to the qualities that you think most attracted you to them, along with any qualities that helped you weather hard times together.

As you write, do you notice any patterns or trends emerging from your relationships? Does it seem to be a mirror of your relationship with your parent, or is it closer to the opposite of your parent (these are the two most common choices)?

Often times reviewing what we gravitate toward in the positive qualities our significant others can shed quite a bit of light on our own insecurities or desires. We may choose someone with certain positive qualities not because such qualities are our perfect complement, but because we have some deep need driving us resulting from some emotional stability that we lack. For example, someone who was tightly controlled by a parent as a child may date someone who is quite laissez faire – or even somewhat checked out – and see that as a great quality in contrast to their childhood environment. In reality, it might be a sign that their significant other isn't that interested in a serious commitment.

Alternatively, daters may also gravitate toward certain positive qualities (e.g. great sense of humor, positive outlook on life) because they truly love that trait in another person. Keep this in mind as you review what you've written, and then create a short list of the characteristics that you *truly* want to find in another person – the qualities you *want* in Your Match.

STEP THREE: Identifying Negative Traits

Similar to what you did in Step Two, you will write down characteristics of each of these people. This time, however, you are writing the person's *negative* traits – at least insofar as his or her relationship to you. For your parent, list any characteristics that made you feel insecure, fearful, or unhappy as you grew up. For people that you dated, what qualities did each have that caused strife in your relationship? (E.g. Belittling, argumentative, condescending, intimidating, cocky, bitter, etc.)

Once again, review what you write for any emerging patterns or trends in your past relationships. If you begin to see a pattern of traits (e.g. choosing men who are particularly picky or fussy, or tend to put you down; choosing women who are clingy and needy) think about what this may say about you.

For example, choosing people who tend to break you down suggests that you may have self-esteem issues, and that you can accept "love" (not very *real* love) from these people because they say negative things about you that you already believe about yourself. Choosing people who are very clingy and needy suggests that you don't believe someone who is a happy and whole person would want to stay with you; you are feeding off of the other person's insecurities which *inevitably* leads to trouble down the line. From any patterns you see emerging, write a statement that encapsulates what you *do not want* in Your Match (and highlight what you need to be especially vigilant to avoid).

STEP FOUR: Identifying Emotions

When you think of each of the six people you've identified, what are the emotions that come to mind? Are they generally positive or negative? Do you feel happily

70

reminiscent, or can you feel anger and bitterness rising to the surface? Are your feelings still very raw, or have your past wounds healed? In order to move forward in healthy ways with new relationships, it's important to recognize where you are in the healing process from the loss (whether it was your choice or not) of past loves. Take a moment to write down five or so emotions that come to mind when you think about your past or present relationship with each person.

Reviewing the emotions you feel toward each of these people will help you to understand where you may still need to do some work or healing. Learning from the painfulness of your past experiences and understanding why you sought or stayed with such people will help to guide you away from making similar choices in the future.

STEP FIVE: Your Old Personals Advertisement

Imagine that you were to write a "want" ad for the kind of person you were looking for. In this ad, you would describe the characteristics of the person, and you might even include how you would want to feel when you were around him or her. In steps Five and Six, that's exactly what you're going to do. You won't specifically use these in crafting your online profile (you'll learn more about the best way to craft a profile soon). Instead, you'll use these to see the kind of message you have been putting out to the world and contrast that with the kind of message you *want* to be putting out to the world.

In this step, you'll actually be crafting your own personal advertisement – but it will be an "Old" personals ad; you'll be describing the kind of person it seems like you have been looking for *in the past* based upon the negative characteristics of your past significant others. To do this, go back and look at the negative characteristics that showed up more than once, the trends that emerged in your selection of who to date, and then craft your old personals ad as I have done below. In the end, it's helpful to be able to have a sense of humor about some of the choices you've made in the past because – and this is the BEST news – you're on a NEW path toward *never making these choices again*!

To help, I've given you the example of what mine looked like six years ago before I began the development of the process through which you WILL find YOUR MATCH!

My Old Personal Ad: *23-year old woman seeks man of questionable or poor moral character. Need not be respectful of my feelings or interested in my goals for the future. I enjoy needy, insecure men, or those who could be described as "Broken" or "Damaged." Bonus points if your insecurity leaves me feeling as though you always have one foot out the door of our relationship. I am religious, but you not only don't have to share my religious views, you need not be religious yourself, nor accepting of my views, nor even respectful of my fundamental belief system. Cheaters welcome – especially if you've cheated with a married woman. I am looking for a passive-aggressive, non-communicator, commitment-phobe with no goals for his life beyond planning his next trip to Vegas. Men with mommy issues are a big plus. If this sounds like you, let's go for coffee and let the mind games begin!*

Are you feeling inspired? (Or maybe sorry for me? If so, don't feel too bad; it all worked out QUITE WELL in the end!) Take a moment to write a paragraph for your own *old* personal ad.

STEP SIX: Your New Personals Advertisement

Writing your old personals ad can be very challenging and sometimes even a bit embarrassing as you have to truly face yourself and the choices you've made. Years back, I felt quite angry at the way I had been used and hurt by men *I had chosen to date.*

With time, I realized that what I was really most upset about was having stayed with these men too long. Have you heard the phrase, "Fool me once, shame on you; fool me twice, shame on me?" I let them fool me time and again, and it was hard to face that the majority of my lingering bad feelings stemmed from my realization that the pain was largely *my fault.* Although that realization is a hard pill to swallow, it brings so much strength because with it comes the truth that each of us has the power to choose who we date and for how long.

> *Empower yourself with the knowledge that YOU are in control of who you date and for how long.*

The good news is that as hard as it is to own up to your role in your own sordid dating history, it will be that much more joyful and exciting to create a new role for yourself as you go forward. You're about to get some fabulous new results because you're about to make some *different choices!*

Take a moment to review the positive qualities you're looking for, and the emotions you want to experience in a relationship and begin crafting your *new* personals ad. This ad will be a great description of Your Match and will set you up well for the subsequent tasks in this section of the book.

Again, to get your creative juices flowing, here is an example that I wrote when looking for My Match and – not coincidentally – it describes him perfectly!

My New Personals Ad: *27-year old woman seeks man of highest moral character. He should be a true optimist, a romantic, and be looking for an emotionally healthy woman with whom to share the rest of his life. He should love God, and be on a constant journey of religious and theological exploration. After God, his first priority will be me and our families. He will dream of being the best father and husband possible, and strive to live each day better than the last. He will be my best friend and, with him, I will always feel a secure connection and deeply loved for exactly the person I am. He will have his own interests and be a best friend to his buddies – the one who can be counted on in the most difficult of situations. If this sounds like you, then send me an email and let's begin our new journey together!*

Ready? Review what you've already prepared and then write Your New Personals Ad. Keep it in a place where you can see it daily. Remind yourself what you are looking for, and make sure with each date that you are not veering off course toward your old path, but keeping your eyes set on your new path toward the love you've always imagined.

Visit the webpage to download and print this worksheet for free!
http://www.meetyourmatchonline.com/how-to-meet-your-match-online-bonus-material/

Chapter 8: Identifying Your Match

When I'm working with clients of Meet Your Match Online, we begin with an initial consultation so that I can understand the client's dating history, likes, dislikes, and deal-breakers. No matter how well I can get to know a client, *the most important part of my process is helping the client get to know him or herself.*

Review this chapter to see what you'll be doing, but do take the time to actually *work it through.* Just as you did in the last chapter, you can visit the Meet Your Match Online website and download and print our proprietary worksheet for free to help you through the process detailed in this chapter.[14]

As I get to know my clients in these first meetings, I find that very few people have actually taken the time necessary to determine exactly who they're looking for. A

---

[14] Worksheet: http://www.meetyourmatchonline.com/how-to-meet-your-match-online-bonus-material/

few people have what they describe as a "type" and others have lists of things they won't tolerate, but almost no one has really drilled down deep enough to truly discover what they need and most desire in someone with whom they will spend the rest of their life.

Doesn't that seem surprising? But then again – have *you* done this work? And I don't just mean daydreaming what your future wife or husband will be like, or putting down height, weight, and hair color preferences on a dating service search engine.

Before you even choose what dating site to use, you should know who you hope to find. Just as it would be lunacy to embark on a long and expensive expedition without having any idea what you hope to find (where would you even start looking?), so too should you avoid starting your search for love with no idea for whom you're looking.

> *Before you start a potentially long and expensive search, you just might want to figure out who you're trying to find.*

The "Open Minded" Approach

Whether we like it or not, we each have a pretty specific set of likes and dislikes. Try as we might to "have an open mind" and not rush to judgment, there are certain traits and qualities that we are each looking for in another person. Clinging too tightly to the idea that we're doing ourselves and the world a favor by being willing to date anyone who crosses our paths helps no one.

For many years I struggled against my own preferences, telling myself I should be more open-minded, and that I could "make it work" with various boyfriends. After all, they were nice, smart, kind, and we had many common interests. I found myself saying the word "potential" quite frequently. It may seem like a nice thing to say about someone, but when it comes to dating it's a dangerous word. It's the kind of word that prophesies five years of wasted time in a relationship that's going nowhere.

> *The Open-Minded Approach is not a workable strategy to finding Your Match.*

In compromising my true desires in my past relationships, I lost what made me special. I felt less than myself. In each such relationship, resentment grew as I felt myself becoming less of who I was, and more of who I believed boyfriends wanted me to be. I spent many unhappy years stuck in this pattern. The "open-minded" approach is not a workable long-term solution. As difficult as life was using this technique for dating (where I could have left the relationship at any time), marriage would have been ten times harder.

However, once I went through process of determining exactly who I was looking for, and ways in which I would never compromise, I was able to sort more quickly through potential dates, and more quickly able to identify who was wrong for me (it never took me longer than two dates after that), and it was only three months later that I found my My Match!

The Targeted Approach

If we're being honest, we can each admit that there *are* certain things we're looking for, and certain things we won't tolerate (the "deal-breakers"). There are ways to say that you need certain things from another person (e.g. the desire to have children together) or that you will never be happy with a certain person (e.g. someone who uses illegal drugs) without being judgmental and harsh. It's personal preference, plain and simple.

Getting to the point that you can clearly state preferences and objections is important, but you have to go further. You have to be able to imagine this person you're looking for, to see your life together, to feel what it would be like to live with them and to share your life. When you get to this point, you will be able to make entire paragraphs using phrases like, "My perfect Match will be _____ and when we're together I will feel _____" [you fill in the blanks].[15]

Clients of Meet Your Match Online work through a guided step-by-step process designed to help each person get in touch with his or her true desires. The primary factor that determines whether our clients are successful in finding love is whether they truly commit to, carry out, and stand by this process.[16] Now it's your turn for this same opportunity for success.

---

[15] Note that I use the phrase "My perfect Match" – this is not to imply that the perfect person for you will be *perfect*, but rather that he or she will be perfect *for you*. The distinction is critical. No one is perfect, and that's good because it would be pretty awful to be held to a standard of perfection and pretty lonely if we would only settle for perfection!

[16] If you'd rather set up an appointment to work through this process together, you can set up your own "Who Is Right For Me?" consultation at http://www.meetyourmatchonline.com/help-with-online-dating-services/

When you've reviewed the process below and are ready to begin, download our content, *print it out*, and GET GOING! You've already taken the first step by getting this book. Let your momentum take you through these next crucial steps. If you don't have the time or computer access to print out the materials and you just can't wait to get started now, here's the abbreviated version:

STEP ONE: Preparation. Make sure that you have allotted enough time to devote to this process. You will need at least an hour or two in a quiet space (i.e. not a coffee shop), where you have a place to sit and a surface to write on. And when I say "write," I actually mean pen or pencil and paper. Not a laptop, desktop, or typewriter.

STEP TWO: Reflection. When you're ready to begin, think about a few times in your life when you have felt very safe, calm, and relaxed. Where were you? What were you doing? Was anyone there with you? Write these memories down. It may sound corny, but by actually bringing up these memories and physically committing them to writing, you are giving yourself a peaceful place to feel safe tapping into your innermost desires. So just do it!

Keep this sheet out with you for the rest of the process. As you do the rest of the steps, call upon your calm and safe memories. Ask yourself whether the picture of the person you are creating will bring you similar feelings of peacefulness, happiness, and calm.

STEP THREE: Must Haves. Create a brainstorm of traits that are very important to you; generate a list of "must haves" in a spouse. *As before, physically write this list down*. Cover every possible trait that is important to you; be as specific as you can. If it is critically important that the person have a certain level of education, include the level of education they must have achieved. If they must be a certain religion, include that religion, and a description of what that means to you (e.g. must they be actively practicing, or just raised in that religion). Assume that if you don't put a trait down, the person won't have it.

Many clients ask at this point, "Should I be including physical traits?" Well, that's up to you. If a physical trait is a requirement and a person without it just won't be Your Match, then put it down. When you're deciding whether to add a physical trait as a requirement, though, I encourage you to think about this person – this love of your life – ten, thirty, and sixty years down the road. Things that *will* change (like hair color, weight, and even height to a certain degree) won't end up being so important as the way the person makes you feel, the way he or she can always make you laugh, or how fantastic a listener he or she is. So consider carefully.

Take time to sit with your list and reflect. Imagine just what the person you are creating would be like and how you would feel to be around them. Refer to the list you created in step two – do the feelings jibe?

STEP FOUR: Create a Narrative. Once you feel content with your list, create a paragraph or two that reads less like a list and more like a narrative. Imagine that what you are creating is exactly how you will be describing your wife or husband to someone someday. The story you are creating will be something you can show to Your Match some day and say, "See? I knew you were out there all along, and I loved you before I knew you."

Whatever it is for you, write it down, sit with it, and see how it feels. Does it feel real? Does it feel too good to be true? If so, you're right on track.

STEP FIVE: Create a Time Frame. In this last step we will create some time frames (i.e. deadlines) for your success. The goal is to be both realistic *and* optimistic. How long from today will you meet this person? Within a week? Within two months? How soon will you be dating? How soon will you be engaged?

Let these time frames drive you, but not control you. Know that in order to meet them, you need to get out there and *meet people*. Lots of people! And as soon as you identify that the person doesn't give you the warm and safe feeling you're looking for or who has a deal-breaker trait, let him or her know he or she isn't the one and *move on!* There's no time to waste.

Some people become concerned with the idea of setting time frames and deadlines for success because they believe something bad will happen if they don't meet these goals. The problem with this thinking is that it implies that such person don't believe he or she can be successful. I will tell you YOU CAN. If you believe you have set an unrealistic deadline for yourself, then change it! Go back and truly think about what you want, and what you can do. *Believe* you can do it.

I was skeptical when I set out on this path too. It's okay to worry that you might not meet your time frame goals provided that it doesn't paralyze you from *trying* to achieve them. I worried, but I worked too. I set my deadlines for when My Match and I would meet, when we'd start dating, get engaged, and even when we would get married. Although I chose not to share these deadlines with My Match, we met *every single one*.

This process WORKS. It absolutely worked for me, and I have read my description to My Match who agrees that it fits him to a T – which he likes very much! It's a wonderful feeling to know that someone chose you

because you are *exactly* what they were looking for.
There's no better reassurance than knowing your partner
didn't settle!

As you go forward with the online dating process,
refer to your list often. Don't judge your decisions. No
one needs to see your list other than you. Take your time
and do this process right. It may be the best investment
of a couple hours you ever made!

Go to http://www.meetyourmatchonline.com/how-to-
meet-your-match-online-bonus-material/
to print our proprietary worksheet for FREE to make this
process easier!

Chapter 9:
Identifying Your
Target Audience

If you've decided that you're ready to date and are looking for a serious relationship, if you know the risks and potential rewards inherent in online dating, and if you have determined exactly who you're looking for, then you are ready to get started actively moving toward finding love. That's a good thing too, as you already have some target time frames and deadlines you're trying to meet!

Initial Considerations

First, you'll need to decide on the right dating service. Since you've already identified who you're trying to meet, finding the right service will be much easier.

Target Audience. It is considerably easier to find the right person once you've completed the exercises set forth in the previous chapters. Once you have an idea of who you want to date (e.g. based on proximity to you, race/ethnicity, religion, or a host of other factors you've already considered) finding the right online dating service is relatively (or comparatively) painless.

If you want to try out online dating for a while, or get a feel for a site before you pay, try the free options (like browsing) available on most pay sites. If you're not too sure about whether you want to be online dating yet, you can give the free sites a try. They're a good place to get some practice communicating and going on casual dates without making a financial commitment (only a time commitment will be required to set up your profile and browse around). When you're ready for a more serious relationship, though, it is probably time to switch to the paid sites like Match.com or eHarmony.com (for general category dating).

One key to determining the right service for you is figuring out your ideal target audience.

It's fine to opt for lesser-trafficked, but more specialized services, but just be aware that you may be drastically reducing your exposure to the available dating pool. [17] If you are *only* looking for people in that demographic, though, it may be worth it to check out that tiny pool first before getting into the large pond. If you don't have luck on the more specific sites, if you have sufficient funds in your dating budget (and additional time to keep up with them) consider using a few sites at the same time.

---

[17] For example, there are services for nearly every religion out there, such as JDate (Jews looking for Jews), along with services that cater to a specific race (BlackPeopleMeet.com), and even sites for "mature" or "senior" singles (OurTime.com).

By getting yourself onto the most heavily trafficked sites, especially heavily trafficked sites that fit your target demographic, you are getting into what is commonly referred to as a "target rich environment." And that's exactly where you want to be.

Budget. When looking at paid membership services offering online dating, working within a budget is an important factor for many online daters. In recent years, the prevalence and popularity of many free sites has grown tremendously, and free online dating is a realistic option for the first time.

Several years ago, some of the only free options were sites like Craigslist, and it seemed as though you were more likely to meet a scammer than a real dating prospect. There is still some truth to the old adage, "You get what you pay for." Sites requiring payment do seem to have a slightly better track record in terms of documenting successful couplings and weeding out people who are simply online to mess with real daters. That's not to say that there aren't predators or posers on paying sites, just that if they're willing to go on a paid site, pay to set up a scam, and leave a paper trail, then they're probably on every free site as well.

Multiple Sites. While I strongly encourage clients to get themselves in target rich environments, some take this to the extreme. Instead of choosing one site that seems like the best fit and easing into things, they'll sign up for Match.com, eHarmony, and every free dating service they can find. Although this scattershot approach will get you in front of a huge ocean of potential candidates, it may

> *Start with one site. Only if you have extra time should you consider layering on more.*

become impossible to keep up with *any* of them. Unless dating is your full time job, investing the time necessary to maintain memberships at three or more different sites is nearly hopeless and certainly overwhelming.

For new daters, think about starting with just one site. After a month, if you feel it's not working for you or that you're not getting the kind of response you want, try a different site or, if you have time, layer the new one over what you're already doing. Don't let things get to the point where you don't even have time to search for or email prospects. No one likes sending out a hopeful email and then having to wait two weeks for a response.

Below is an overview of several popular dating sites. These do not comprise the entirety of what is out there, but rather serve to give the 10,000 foot view of some popular sites that are available:

POPULAR ONLINE DATING SERVICE WEBSITES[18]
(Alphabetically)

Site Name: **Catholic Match**

Description: The largest and most respected online service for singles in the Catholic community.
Number of Registered Users: Over 2 Million. [19]
Monthly Cost: Basic membership is free, but additional features available to paid members. One month for $24.95 (rates dependent on subscription length).
Premium Service Available: Yes. A paid subscription is needed to communicate with other users, but the free service is

---

[18] Information and statistics gathered from various websites. Readers should check with each site for the latest pricing and policies.
[19] http://www.top10bestdatingsites.com/CatholicDatingWebsites-Comparison?kw=catholic%20dating%20site&c=7680220267&t=search&p=&m=e&a=1&gclid=CPaHu-ro9qgCFRs5gwodv1yuVA

available to run searches and browse who is using the service.

Same-Sex Dating: Not likely.

Website Address: www.catholicmatch.com

Site Name: **Chemistry**

Description: A sister-site of Match.com; members are matched with other members based on their profiles. Unlike Match.com, users cannot search for their own matches. Instead, Chemistry searches for you using The Chemistry Profile^{TM} personality assessment, which (according to them) identifies the key factors that lead to truly successful relationships.

Number of Registered Users: 11 Million registered users.[20]

Monthly Cost: $49.95 (rates dependent on subscription length).

Premium Service Available: Yes. Users can see more matches than non-paying members (who see only 5 matches per day).

Same-Sex Dating: Yes.

Website Address: www.chemistry.com

Site Name: **Compatible Partners**

Description: eHarmony's service for same-sex relationships.

Number of Registered Users: Unknown. It is a relatively new service.

Monthly Cost: Between $19.95 and $59.95 depending on length of subscription purchased.[21]

Same-Sex Dating: Yes (the site is specifically for same-sex relationships).

Website Address: www.compatiblepartners.net

Site Name: **eHarmony**

Description: Dating site focused on matching users with other users (rather than letting users browse to find each other). This service has a lengthy pre-screening Q&A

---

[20] http://www.confirio.com/blog/?p=19. October 23, 2010.

[21] http://www.eharmony.com/press/release/19

process using personality tests designed to match users based on compatibility, and has features that can guides the conversation and get-to-know you process (although users can also opt to "Fast Track" their dating process to communicate freely sooner).

Number of Registered Users/Active Members: 37 Million registered users; 750,000 active (as of 2009).[22]

Monthly Cost: $59.99 (rates dependent upon subscription length).

Premium Service Available: There is free service available, but a subscription is required to use most features.

Same-Sex Dating: No. Compatible Partners is eHarmony's site for same-sex relationships.

Website Address: www.eharmony.com

Site Name: **Lavalife**

Description: One of the oldest dating companies in the world.

Number of Registered Users: Unknown.

Monthly Cost: The pricing structure is somewhat confusing. Research indicates that the free membership allows you to search for singles, create profiles, post pictures to the site, and respond to emails and text messages. For $34.99 per month, you can send unlimited instant messages and emails and see who has viewed your profile.[23]

Same-Sex Dating: Yes.

Website Address: www.lavalife.com

Site Name: **Match.com**

Description: One of the biggest online singles meeting services in the world.

Number of Registered Users/Active Members: As of 2009 reports, there were 96 Million registered users and 1,377,000 active members.[24]

---

[22] http://www.confirio.com/blog/?p=19. October 23, 2010.

[23] http://freeonlinedatingtips.net/dating-sites/lavalife-review

[24] http://www.confirio.com/blog/?p=19. October 23, 2010.

Monthly Cost: $34.99/month (rates dependent upon subscription length).
Premium Service Available: There is free service available, but a subscription is required to use most features.
Same-Sex Dating: Yes.
Website Address: www.match.com

Site Name: **OkCupid**

Description: Uses answers from user-generated questions to find matches that conform to a user's stated preferences.
Number of Active Members: As of 2010, 5.6 Million.[25]
Monthly Cost: None.
Premium Service Available: Yes. Service is free to join, search, message, and chat. Non-essential features like sponsored profiles are available to paying members. (Upgrade is $9.99, with a discount available for students.)
Same-Sex Dating: Yes.
Website Address: www.okcupid.com

Site Name: **OurTime**

Description: One of the newest online dating services, this site caters to the 50+ age group and is owned by the same group that owns Match.com. By combining the membership of multiple existing dating sites, OurTime is the world's largest dating community specifically targeted to singles over the age of 50.
Number of Registered Users: Over one million at its launch.
Monthly Cost: $20 for just one month, down to $12 if you buy a six month membership.
Same-Sex Dating: Yes.
Website Address: www.OurTime.com

Site Name: **PlentyOfFish**

Description: One of the most popular dating sites in the United States and United Kingdom.

---

[25] *Id.*

Number of Registered Users: 23 Million.[26]
Monthly Cost: None.
Premium Service Available: Yes. Users can take a test and pay
    a fee to be upgraded to the status of "serious member."
    (Upgrade at $88.20 per quarter.)
Same-Sex Dating: Yes.
Website Address: www.plentyoffish.com

Site Name: **Zoosk**

Description: Dating site, often focusing on less-serious
    relationships, which differentiates itself from other
    sites by tapping into and linking with social network-
Number of Registered Users: 50 Million.[27]
Monthly Cost: You can log on and create a profile for free; sub-
    scriptions are $29.95 (rates dependent upon
    subscription length), and allow users to get full access
    to send and receive messages and winks, chat with
    friends, find out who viewed their profile, etc.
Premium Service Available: Yes.
Same-Sex Dating: Yes.
Website Address: www.zoosk.com

Offline Dating Services

    Many clients are occasionally hesitant to jump
right into online dating and find that they are looking for
some more "in-person" dating experience first. Many
have considered services like "It's Just Lunch" and
"Events and Adventures." These in-person services
(where daters meet live with other daters for various
events like lunch or wine tasting) can be quite costly and
extremely frustrating and disappointing for many who
pay their hefty fees and sign their cumbersome contracts.

---

[26] *Id.*

[27] http://www.zoosk.com/about.php. June 5, 2011.

It's Just Lunch does not post a cost on its website, though users report its annual membership cost to be between $1,100 to $2,200 depending on the region.[28] The organization's intent – which is noble, to be sure – is to set up like-minded business people living and working in the same areas in the hope that they will be compatible. Users are personally interviewed, which provides some additional safety over online dating in that there is at least one human screening people before you meet them. The service generally promises 12-14 lunch meetings (with different people).

> *The main flaw with this service is that daters say they want one thing, but actually want another.*

The main flaw with this service is that many daters *say* they want one thing, but *actually* want another. (We touched on this briefly in our previous chapter addressing dating the wrong "type.") Most likely, such daters are not even consciously aware of their fickle nature.[29] Thus, when the service matches you up with the type of person you've described wanting you're never going to be satisfied. In contrast, (most) online dating services allow you to browse users and perhaps contact someone you wouldn't have otherwise expected to be attracted to.

Events and Adventures, similar to It's Just Lunch, does not post its cost online, nor is it readily disclosed

---

[28] Source:
http://www.consumeraffairs.com/dating_services/just_lunch_women.html (gathered May 31, 2011).
[29] Online dating services like Match.com get around this problem by creating algorithms that pay close attention to the profiles that users browse and contact, rather than just the people users *claim* to be interested in. It's one of the reasons they are so successful!

from a phone call. Online reviewers of the service claim that it costs $2,000/year and you cannot get out of the contract unless you rescind it within three days of signing up. The primary complaint with these services tends to be that you see the same group of 7-10 people at every event and if you don't click with any of them (e.g. if they are all 20 years younger or older than you) then you're pretty much out of luck and stuck in the service until your contract expires. To add salt to the wounds, users report there are often additional charges to attend many events over and above the hefty cost of membership.

I strongly discourage clients from using this type of service. Being required to sign up for such an expensive service with a *year-long* commitment, and no prior knowledge about types of people you will be meeting almost never works out.

Mutual Friend. In response to the complaints about dating options in the Northwest, I recently started a one-to-one matchmaking company called "Mutual Friend" (www.MutualFriendMatchmaking.com). The matchmaking services focuses exclusively on intellingent, Northwest singles who haven't yet met their match. We keep costs *very low* for clients, have no lengthy contracts to sign, month-to-month subscriptions available, and answer all questions up front about our services. We are even offering FREE membership for those who qualify.[30] If you're not in the Northwest, check around in your nearest major city for a similar service. The best part about using a matchmaking company is that they will meet with you in person (the good ones) and get to know you and exactly who you're looking for. It can be one more great way to get yourself in front of the *right* audience.

---

[30] See more about this in the second Free Offer at the end of the book.

Practice Activities

For my clients who just aren't ready to try online dating, or who have tried it and want a more in-person approach (or practice), I often recommend a round of speed dating for some good "one-on-one with a stranger" practice.

Speed Dating events may be sponsored by organizations such as churches or private firms and generally ask that you register for the event in advance. Typically, groups of about 20 men and 20 women come to the event in order to meet other singles. Singles get to meet everyone in the room and find out if they're interested in seeing each other for a date outside the confines of the speed dating event.

The usually starts with mingling, and then the 20 couples sit down at 20 tables and talk for about three minutes. The host rings a bell (or otherwise signifies the time is up) and the men move to the next table. After an hour, each man has spent three minutes with each woman. On a sheet of paper (or online later) each person reports who he or she would be interested in seeing again. If there are any matches, the host will pair the two up for another meeting. The couples take it from there!

> *Speed Dating can provide excellent one-on-one practice for nervous daters.*

Most big cities have these events in abundance, and you can often find speed dating events that are targeted toward an age group or religious preference. They usually aren't too expensive either. Although I don't find speed dating to be particularly effective in meeting Your Match, it does work well for clients who just need a bit of extra practice getting comfortable meeting strangers.

The fact that they're only meeting each person for three minutes and never have to see them again provides a certain amount of safety to practice your "elevator pitch" and prepare you for future meetings with other potential matches.

Some other offline dating ideas include checking out the "Meet Up" groups in your area. These are groups usually formed by private citizens with common interests. They range from scuba diving, to rock climbing, to political interests/activism, to wine tasting, and everything in between. It's really quite a mixed bag of individuals, and the groups can have high turnover, but the concept is great. Even if you don't make a love connection, you have the chance to expand your network of friends and meet people with at least *one* common interest.

If you're not sure what options are best for you, contact me at Laura@MeetYourMatchOnline.com to learn more or to set up a consultation to design a targeted dating approach customized just for you, and appropriate for your dating budget.

PART THREE: YOUR ONLINE PERSONA

Now that you've identified who you're looking for and where you should look, it's time to put finger to keyboard and get yourself out there!

In Part Three you will learn: (1) how to create the perfect profile to attract *just* who you're looking for, (2) how to write the often-dreaded essay section that will catch Your Match's eye, and (3) how to avoid and fix common profile mistakes.

Chapter 10: Creating A Profile to Attract Your Match

Once you have decided what online dating service you're going to try, it will be time to set up your profile. Depending upon the service, this may require several hours of commitment. Make sure to give yourself enough time to get completely through the process of crafting your profile – don't take it on at a time when you're too busy and burn out before you even start!

This initial step *must not be rushed*. Many sites do allow you to go back and make changes about your preferences later, but some sites require completion of a lengthy Q & A section that cannot be changed without re-taking the entire questionnaire. Give yourself enough time to do these personality and chemistry questionnaires correctly to make sure they are connecting you with the best possible matches.

Even if you're signing up for a site that does allow you to go make changes (like Match.com), take your time to do it right the first time. Many daters are just excited to go browse, so they rush the profile to get to the browsing stage. The danger here is that you will forget to go back, or you'll be getting responses from other users so you won't bother to re-craft your profile. Then all your hard work in determining who you are looking for and communicating that to others goes down the drain! Additionally, you may get more "publicity" when you're a new user. So your first impression to your potential matches out there is a BAD one if you're profile is in lame shape.

> *NEVER post a profile that is incomplete.*

Do it right once and be done. DO NOT post a profile that is incomplete. If it's not ready, wait until you have more time to finish! If your pictures are horrific, don't post them or your profile! If you have to do your profile in bits and pieces, make sure you keep it hidden until it's totally ready to go. If you're rushing because you want to get on to the browsing, just hide your profile, come back to it when you have more time, and browse away.

Step 1: Profile Creation Basics

Creating a captivating profile is critically important to attracting the right person. Even if you're able to find him or her, he or she may not respond to you if you've done a lousy job of creating your profile. Depending on the online dating service you're using, this may be a guided process in which you have little chance to be creative or think outside the box, or you may have nearly total freedom to state who you are and what you're looking for. Use the advice below as appropriate for the site you've selected.

Focus on selecting a good (or at least not terrible) screen name, concocting a catchy opening line, uploading a strong profile picture, and weaving a succinct picture for visitors to your profile of who you are and who you're looking for. Avoid typographical errors at all costs! Also stay away from sexual references, over-sharing about your personal situation, and *any mention or photos of exes* or discussion of past relationships.

The "DOs" and "DON'Ts" of Choosing a Screen Name

Although it may not seem important, a screen name is one of the first things the other person sees. An otherwise innocuous profile may deter contacts because of a truly terrible choice of screen name. Here are some good rules of thumb:

- o   DO reference something you enjoy (like nature or sports);
- o   DO reference a nickname (provided the nickname doesn't violate another rule listed below)
- o   DO reference a city you love or live in;
- o   DO reference a positive quality trait of yours (e.g. tough, rugged, sweet, caring, loyal);

- o   DO NOT reference alcohol, drugs, prostitution, witchcraft, or being a player/easy;
- o   DO NOT reference anything overtly sexual in nature (including references to sex acts); and
- o   DO NOT flaunt your wealth.

I have included a (slightly modified, to protect anonymity) list of *real* screen names for comparison:[31]

Bad Screen Names	Acceptable Screen Names
Hello12345 (too generic)	Chris1483 (generic, but not too generic)
NewEx4u	Luvstheoutdoors
PympOlympics	VikingsFan
RedCherry (too sexual)	Photographybuff
RetardedApe (awful)	SeattleSailor
Keg69 (double whammy – references alcohol and sexual overtones)	FoodieHiker
BMWFan	Scoots1218
FerrariLuvvr	TrueFealty63
MonkeySpank	Loves2GardenInRain
Freakshow	GreenEyedGoddess
GinNTonic	CountryFirstWoman
PokherPlaya (the terrible trifecta – referencing gambling, being a player, and a sexual reference)	BrunetteTriathlete
	SassyLittleLassie
HookupJR	LoyalLawyerLady
Lucifer (creepy/scary)	

Catchy Subject Lines & Openers

Some dating sites allow you a headline, while others just have a single free-write area in which you are able to write whatever you feel like. At best, you'll come up with something clever to put here; humor is always good, as is a statement or question that draws a reader in and makes them want to learn more. At worst, however,

---

[31] Each of the bad names is a slightly modified version of a screen name of someone who actually contacted me. If any of these is someone's *actual* screen name, I am not talking about you, as these have all been modified from the originals. That said, if I were you I would re-think my screen name choice if you're in the "bad" category...

you'll put something so stupid or offensive that will be sufficiently off-putting to drive would-be winkers or emailers away. If you can't think of something to write, just try a short, simple summary of yourself. Here are some real examples of the good, bad, and the workable:

GOOD/FUNNY LINES:

- "Looking for a new hiking partner!"
- "I love adventure! Want to try sky diving with me?"
- "Let me show off my baking skills for you!"
- "I'm looking for someone who can catch my eye from across the room, and stay up all night talking!"
- "How would we do at the Amazing Race?"
- "My mom thinks I'm special. And she doesn't like backtalk."
- "Time Traveler seeks wife."
- "Next week is no good; the Jonas Brothers are in town." [From a man. Good, as long as he's kidding.]

BAD LINES:

- "I like Doritos. Soooo, that's happening." [What?]
- "Life is to [sic] short to waste on people that suck." [So negative.]
- "I wish to meet present the man. Strongly and tender which would grow fond of me all heart." [If you don't speak English, get lots of help with your profile.]
- "Cat lover from another mother."
- "I look hot and you should too."
- "Hi there."
- "Who's ready for advernture." [Don't make a typo-graphical error in your header.]
- "Can you keep up with me?" [Intimidating; potentially off-putting.]

- "Insert witty comment here." [*Everyone* is using this line.]

MEDIOCRE LINES:

- "Looking to meet nice, active and confident young professional or student."
- "I'm a sucker for a smile!" [Generic.]
- "I like to laugh and have a good time." [Who doesn't?]
- "Imagination is more important than knowledge. Knowledge is limited. Imagination encircles the world. – Albert Einstein" [If you use a quote, make sure to tie its relevance in within your profile.]
- "Anything worth having is worth working hard for."
- "I'm some kind of jock/nerd hybrid."
- "Honesty is the only policy."
- "Experience is the most brutal teacher. You get the test first and the lesson second."

Describing Yourself

How to really sell any free-write portion of the profile is covered in depth in the next chapter. That said, there are many places in the profile (darn near the whole thing) that require self-description. Use these guidelines in creating those sections.

Before writing a self-descriptive portion of your profile, spend some time brainstorming. Use this portion of your profile to answer some questions before they're asked. Show all the *positive* ways that you stand out from the crowd. Try this exercise, writing down the answer to each of the following questions:

○ What do you think your best five qualities are?

o   What makes you different from any random person on the street? What would a stranger be happily surprised to learn about you?

o   If we asked your five closest friends to each tell us one story about you that captures who you are, what story would each tell?

As you go through this process, do any common themes emerge? Remember, you're trying to present your best self to a stranger. It's often a fine line to walk between putting your best self forward and bragging.

At Meet Your Match Online, we offer assistance in the creation of profiles, and also offer a service where we will review and critique your profile for you, creating feedback and suggested changes. If you aren't able to use our service, *at the very least* get someone to read through it for you and let you know how it comes across. See if they can tell you what message you are sending out – does that match what you were trying to do?

Describing Your Mr. or Ms. Right

Your goal in creating your own profile should be to catch the eye and capture the attention of Your Match, so you'll want to make sure to give your readers a good description of just who you're looking to meet. Remember, your objective is not to attract every subscriber to the service – *just the ones who would be a good fit for you.*

> *The objective is not to attract every subscriber – just the ones that would be a good fit for you.*

To help you with this portion, refer to your previous work determining who you are trying to find. Write your profile as if you are trying to win over the person you describe in that exercise.

As a self-check when you've finished this portion (and to determine whether your description comes across well), think of yourself and the person you've described at age 80. You'll be old, saggy, and crinkly, but will you still be happy with this person? Will they have all the internal qualities that will keep you in love over the years?

It is also useful to spend a portion of your essay section discussing what you're looking for in a long term relationship. Create a verbal picture of what a serious relationship would look like to you. (E.g. Would it be a lot of travel? Lots of clubbing? Do you love to stay home and read a good book by the fireplace? Do you want someone to go on long car trips with, to sail the open waters with, or do you get motion sick?) By describing what your life would be like with this person, you give them an opportunity to dream with you and see if your dreams are compatible.

Choosing a Primary Photo

Our research has revealed that photographs are the number one factor considered by both men and women when deciding whether to contact someone. That is to say, if the photographs are terrible, it's nearly impossible for the text to salvage your profile. Perhaps this is why some online dating services won't show you pictures unless you have signed up for their service. And yet it seems at least half of the primary photos online violate one of my laws for posting photos.

Entire books could be written about the ways that people go wrong in their photos. I won't go into the hundreds of ways here, but here are ten Meet Your Match

Online Laws[32] that, if followed, should keep you on the right track when taking or choosing a primary photo:

1. **Your face shall be clearly visible in the photo**. What we're trying to accomplish is having a clear photo of your face, the way it looks today, visible to the world. Don't hide behind giant sunglasses, a weird, trendy veil, a Kentucky Derby hat, or some trying-to-be-artsy shadow. Show yourself! Ideally, in a well lit location, turned toward the camera, cropped from about your chest up.

2. **The photo shall be of you and you alone**. One of the most embarrassing things that can happen when you add others to the primary photo is the person contacting you thinks he or she is going to meet your friend – *not you!* This happens far more than it should. It's so awkward, so just avoid the confusion. If you have a picture where you look great, but it has your friends in it, either crop it or save it for the collateral photos.

3. **The photo shall be a current photo of you**. This is especially important for the primary photo. Choose a photo that is no more than a year (or two if you still look the same) old, and reflects a close approximation to how you would look if you went on a date that day. If there have been any major changes (e.g. you shaved your head or gained/lost 80 pounds) you MUST let your date know before you meet.[33] If anything, you want him or her to feel

---

[32] As an attorney, I'm wild about the opportunity to make some laws here.
[33] I once dated a man who had lost 75 pounds in the six months prior to our first meeting. His pictures were current and he looked the same on the date, but when I eventually saw pictures of him from only 6 months before, he

pleasantly surprised when they meet you – not shocked and disappointed (and potentially deceived).

4. **You shall be fully clothed in the photo.** Wear a shirt, some pants...the whole deal. Yes, even if you have great abs or are otherwise God's gift to men or women. Sadly, I also have to say this: Under no circumstances should any picture in your profile include photos of genitalia (yours or otherwise).

5. **You shall not be wearing a costume.** As fun as it is to see your playful side, save it for the collateral photos. Unless your normal, everyday self wears a wizard costume (yes, there's a true story behind this one), don't bring it out of the closet for the primary photo. Try something business casual or from a relaxed "weekend version" of yourself.

6. **You shall not be holding a container of alcohol in the photo.** It's not classy, and it will generally not be your best look. Consider that one day you may show your kids the photo that eventually won their mom's/dad's heart. *Worst case scenario:* If it's your absolute best photo ever, at least crop the hand holding the PBR out of the photo.

7. **You shall be sober in the photo.** See reasons in the previous Law.

---

was unrecognizable. The strangest part was that he had no idea he looked so different to others. The lesson there is that we often don't have good perspective on ourselves. So just choose *current* photos and avoid any potential embarrassment in a date setting later.

8. **You shall not, under any circumstances, post a photo taken of you in a bathroom**. I feel like this shouldn't need explanation, but there are SO MANY bathroom shots out there. Even if you live somewhere that cameras freeze when they go outside, and you have to take the picture inside, there are lots of other rooms available in your house, or maybe even other indoor locations besides your home. For the best lighting and an interesting background to your shot, though, I highly recommend having your picture taken outdoors.

> *You should not, under any circumstances, post a picture of you taken in a bathroom.*

9. **You shall have someone else take the photo**. When you can't even scrounge up one photo that someone else took of you, this tells the world, "I don't have a single friend in the whole world, and I've never ever done anything worth taking a picture of." I highly doubt this is true, of course, but it's the message that is sent.

10. **You shall smile**.[34] Really. Do it. Who are you, the Mona Lisa? Forget intrigue and mystique and just *smile*. If you have insecurity issues with your teeth, deal with that separately because if things work out, Your Match is eventually going to see your teeth.

---

[34] My Match broke this Law. He didn't smile in a single picture, and that *almost* kept me from meeting him, but he seemed to have a good sense of humor in every other way so I gave it a try (thank God). Turns out he has a *lovely* smile, but just doesn't love to smile for pictures.

In sum, a good profile picture is NOT a picture of your abs you took yourself shirtless in the bathroom mirror one drunken afternoon five years ago when you were totally ripped with your camera phone in one hand and a beer in the other. This breaks just about every rule, except perhaps the requirement that you smile, which we can't see since your head isn't even in the picture.

Choosing Collateral Photos

How Many Photos? One of the most common questions I receive about collateral photos is *how many* a dater should have. I recommend between 4-8 photos that are no more than 1-2 years old. (As in the primary photo, if you look very different now than you did two years ago, stick with pictures that show your *current* look.)

You want enough pictures that your potential date can really get a feel for what you look like, what activities you enjoy, and how your look changes over the course of a year (same hair style, or handlebar mustache every few months?). Each photo should be from a different event, and should include you. Many daters make the mistake of including 10 photos they took of their loveable cat, or of scenery on their latest hike. Potential dates want to see YOU; you can show off your photography skills down the road.

Include about 4-8 photos that are no more than 1-2 years old.

What Should I Be Doing? Include pictures of you engaged in the things you talk about enjoying in other parts of your profile. Among other benefits, it adds to your credibility. If you say you love to sail and you've navigated a boat through the Panama Canal, having a photo of that will really drive the point home. In contrast, if you say you love to sail, but you've never set foot on a boat (and rarely even bathe) you're going to mislead people and that is NEVER a good way to start a relationship.

Ideally, each photo should represent a different facet of your personality. For example, a nice grouping might include pictures of you hiking, traveling, gardening, spending Thanksgiving with your family, and bowling with your friends.

May I Include Others In the Photo? As long as you have several pictures where you're alone (and your primary photo only shows you), it's just fine to include some pictures with other people in them. Whenever possible, try to point out which person in the photo is you. It may be obvious to you, but to a complete stranger your face isn't all that recognizable. But never, ever, *ever* include a photo of you with an ex-boyfriend or ex-girlfriend.[35]

Advice for Men. You should have VERY FEW, if any pictures of yourself with women within 20 years of your age because women may assume that it's an ex-girlfriend, which will lead to the assumption that you're still hung up on her, and she'll disregard your profile and move on. (You may *consider* including a photo with nieces, sisters, or grandmas IF you clarify in a caption who they are, but it's still a gamble.) Just avoid having any female friends in those pictures entirely, though, if you can.

And, as previously mentioned, keep your shirt on. Many men like it when women show a little skin in their photos, but the converse is infrequently true. Women of-

---

[35] Even if it's your best picture of yourself, and even if you explain that you've broken up with the other person. It's a huge turnoff for potential dates.

ten assume that men with too many skin shots are conceited and cocky. A good rule is to have no more than one swimsuit picture – if you must have one – and make it legitimate (i.e. if you're stating that you love to sailboard or surf, you can get away with having *one* photo doing those activities). Men are also the biggest culprits of being drunk (or actively drinking) in photos, but please note that women's descriptions of what they're seeking in long-term partners rarely include "always super drunk."

Finally, of note, a November 2010 article from Men's Health cites OKCupid research indicating that men may get good responses from women if they post a photo where they're doing something interesting while neither smiling nor looking at the camera. Although I recommend an inviting smile for your primary photo, go ahead and try a non-smiler for a collateral photo.

Advice for Women. It is true that women who show more skin tend to get more responses from guys. However, it is *not* true that these responses are the *kind* of responses you want; they're usually not from quality men looking for long term relationships. So ladies, you should keep your clothes on too. Don't give it away for free. Also, there are tons of creepers out there. And your boss. Posting photos that are too revealing tend to draw in the predators like moths to a flame.

Also, in contrast to my advice for men, I recommend that you include a picture or two of yourself with men in your peer group. As a general rule, guys like to think you're attractive to the opposite sex, and tend not to react jealously to these photos. But even so – still no ex-boyfriends.

Chapter 11: Writing Your Match's Dream Essay

People tend have an incredibly difficult time with the free-write section of the profile... to the point that it seems to nearly cripple them. They are left in a quivering ball on the floor having only typed "I'm no good at this kind of thing." Or, "my friend made me join this site, and I'm not sure what I'm doing here." FAIL!

If you're among the quivering masses, you're in plentiful company. Culturally, we're taught not to toot our own horns, so writing about how great we are and why someone should date us doesn't always come naturally. In this chapter you will learn everything you need to know to nail the essay section and any additional free-write areas of your profile. Here are the Meet Your Match Online *Supreme Laws* of Essay Writing:

Supreme Law of Essay Writing For Men

Talk about a few accomplishments, a few pastimes, and *talk about what you see for your future*. Women love to see that you have drive, passion, and vision for your life, and we want to know everything you're willing to share about these topics.

Supreme Law of Essay Writing For Women

Let men know that you are *complete and happy as you are*. (Note: If you're entering the dating world, this statement should be true!) Unless you're a complete person without them, you will almost invariably come across as needy or desperate. It's a bit of a cliché, but if you're not happy with yourself, no one else will be able to make you happy. Men love to see that you're a thriving human being – even without them. Show him that you aren't and will not be dependent on him for happiness and he'll run to you like a kid to an ice cream truck.

Seven Laws You Must Obey to Rule the Essay

1. **Give it the time it deserves**. One of the biggest mistakes many online dating service users make is underestimating the importance of the "essay" or "free-write" portion of an online profile. With many online dating services, by the time you get to the essay, you may have already been working on crafting your profile, taking personality tests, and filling out information about yourself for hours. Despite your inevitable fatigue, DO NOT POST YOUR PROFILE UNTIL YOU FULLY COMPLETE YOUR ESSAY SECTION. And when I say fully complete your essay, that includes:

    a) Creating a well-thought out description of yourself which includes a descriptive story or humorous reference;

112

b) Adding detail about what sort of man or woman you are looking for (which you will have a clear vision of after having completed the exercises laid out in Part Two of the book); and

c) Having someone else review what you have done.

Many people have trouble with every single one of these rules, but each instruction is critically important. My research has shown that people, women especially, will move on from a profile of a person to whom they otherwise would have written simply based on dislike of what the person had to say, or the feeling that the essay was slapped together thoughtlessly.

Remember, it doesn't have to be a novel, just create a length you are comfortable with (usually 2-3 paragraphs). Include enough information and detail to give someone an idea of you but not so much so that they don't still have to contact you to learn more.

2. **Proofread, proofread, proofread.** The most commonly cited reason given in our recent research for disregarding a potential Match's profile is mistakes in spelling or grammar.

3. **Don't talk about anything overly personal (especially exes).** Everyone has some amount of baggage, and it will all eventually come out if the relationship works out. Even so, there's no reason to lay all your personal damage on someone in the section where you're supposed to be selling yourself.

4. **Avoid neediness.** Neediness comes in many different shapes and sizes. Often men are needy in an "I need a housekeeper/cook/laundry lady" kind of way. Or they will ask for "a great foot rub or back rub." Uh, how about if we see if we can share a pizza and conversation before you try to get me to clean your house. In contrast, women tend to be more emotionally needy. They'll ask for someone to keep them company, make them happy, or emotionally fulfill them. Ladies – men worry enough about trying to impress us just by taking us out to dinner. Let's not pin our hopes, dreams, and eternal happiness on them too.

5. **Be confident, but not cocky.** Confidence is attractive. Let others in on what makes you so great and let people know what you love to discuss or do in your free time. Cockiness is a huge turn-off, though. You can stay on the safe side of the line between these two by sharing stories of your triumphs and *how they changed you*, rather than simply listing your life's accomplishments.[36]

6. **Mention deal-breakers, but avoid laundry lists.** Listing too many qualifications the other person must possess may cause them to self-select out of contacting you entirely. Do state deal-breakers (if you're *sure* they're deal-breakers, like wanting to have kids vs. not wanting kids). Otherwise, avoid coming across as "picky" as much as you can. You'll have plenty of time to grill your date more subtly and effectively if you get to meet in person.

---

[36] You'll see an example of a bragging/cocky email below from the first person I dated (the mountain climbing doctor). It's pretty easy to spot cockiness when you're reading someone else's profile but do review your own profile with this same critical eye.

7. **Err on the side of being vague**. Studies from Harvard, Boston University, and MIT agree that when it comes to essay sections of dating profiles, less is more because people "mistake vagueness for attractiveness, filling in the missing details in ways that suit their own desires," psychologist Robert Epstein explains in an online dating article for *Scientific American.*

Lessons from Real Profiles

I am including a few excerpts from online daters who have contacted me over the years, along with some other "gems" excerpted from profiles. *You should not necessarily model yours after these, as many are examples of what NOT to do.* I'll say it again because it's THAT hard to believe – ALL of these are verbatim quotes from *real profiles:*

Profile 1 – What Language Is That?: *"I the fine girl with a brilliant smile. Very loving to communicate to whom be on any theme. It is very interesting to me to learn that that new from friends. I very much like to grow up various kinds of colors. And still to me to like quiet music under which is silent is possible to calm down and easy to have a rest after what be affairs."*

Lessons: This is a mess. A complete and total mess. If you don't speak English, or not well, have someone who does help you with your profile. It's important that your matches know your language barriers/deficits, but it's also important that they can understand what you're trying to convey. You can have whoever is helping you communicate that you're still learning English to the recipient of your communications. This profile needs to be trashed and started over, though. Maybe burned, the ashes doused with lighter fluid, and burned again. It's a train wreck.

115

Profile 2 – The Overshare: *"Myself I'm very honest, it gets me in trouble all the time. I love physical/ mentally intense activities. I will play all day, if you want, but can also sit in a bookstore reading for hours. I was a super science & art freak but am a natural with sports too. I don't fake what I am, what you see is what you get with me, no games. I'm unselfish, will not hesitate to help you, even if it means risking my life. Don't take advantage of this trait please. I love to play & laugh, I'm a goof ball. I love diff cultures/people. Very flexible & adaptive. LOVE to laugh and joke around. Blah, blah, yada, yada... I've only been in 3 intimate relationships in my life, which means I've had sex and kissed only 3 women so if your looking for lots of experience I'm not the one for you (was really shy). All 3 relationships ended great. I still play tennis with my last lover but she has found another man and isn't allowed to play with me anymore :'(A little jealousy is OK, but when you can't trust each other to hang out with friends, not cool. My date/lover/partner/friend... As long as your INTELLIGENT, beautiful, althletic, good humor and like to cuddle I'll be happy. You must like animals, especially the ones that go "Woof, woof". If you don't mind being licked allot, that would be a big plus. :-) Getting a dog as soon as I move from my tiny apartment. Don't worry I'll pet you too if we date *wink* And how can I forget, MUST be honest. To some things up, I'm looking for a great woman to share my time with. Hope to find a good friend first, then in the long run, someone to share emotional & physical intimacy. 4 weeks into this match thing I must add... I'm not looking for women that do hard drugs, No french kissing me on the first date (just as intimate to me as sex), or booty calls hrs after first date (I LOVE sex too, but can we get to know each other first?). Getting wasted first time turns me off. Accurate pic would help :-/"*

Lessons: This profile is all over the place in every possible way. It's just one run on paragraph without any structure. Sure, it has some good features (concrete examples of what he enjoys here and there) but it is also impossible to follow, WAY too sexual, exaggerating (talking about dying for you), riddled with spelling and grammar errors, and conveys the message that whoever wrote it just kind of spewed out whatever was on his mind at that moment. A good sign that your profile is not sufficiently polished is if it contains the words "blah blah" or "yadda yadda" – or both. Although this essay might be a good brainstorm activity for what to include in your *real* essay, this dater needs to scrap this and start over.

Profile 3 – Good, But Not Great: *"I live in Seattle and am really loving friends and work, but I would like to meet that special someone! I occasionally like to go out and get drinks, but I also like to stay in on a cold night, cook dinner, drink wine and watch movies. I love being outdoors; spending a weekend camping and hiking is refreshing when you live in a city. My family lives nearby and I try to see them every week. My brother and I are very close... My friends are like family to me, so I am hoping to meet someone who is comfortable with themselves and can hang out with new people. I love to laugh, be with people I love, do yoga, try out new recipes, discover new places, and am hoping to get better at skiing!*

"I am looking for a guy that has great values and is close with his family. I want someone who treats me with respect, is a gentleman and can be my best friend. He should make me feel comfortable, be able to laugh at anything and have a funny, spontaneous side. I am also pretty drama free and am hoping to keep it that way. Let me know if this is you :)"

Lessons: This woman has done a great job with her profile, but there's room for improvement. She's keeping it short and sweet, and giving concrete examples of activities that she enjoys (camping and hiking), her priorities (family and friends), and some ideas about her future (learning to ski).

Areas where she could improve would be cutting out clichés ("I like to be outdoors," "I'm hoping to meet someone comfortable with themselves," "I love to laugh") and replacing them with more concrete examples. She could include what her favorite hike has been, or a few sentences about the funniest thing that's happened to her while camping. She could add something about an upcoming trip she's training for or hoping to take. She could also stand to be more specific about who she's looking for. For example, what does it mean that he is close with his family? I have found that means VASTLY different things to people (some guys call Mom every day, others see her once a year – both said they were "close"). This dater's profile is markedly improved from the previous two, however. She's headed in the right direction, and just might need one more round of editing.

Profile 4 – It's My World, You're Just Hoping To Live In It: *"Puckish is a good descriptive word for me, I'll stick with it. You might have to look it up, I did, it's not used much. I tend to swear when I'm happy about something, and appreciate creative or innovative use of profanity, it is an art, or skill, one must hone.*

"I'm involved in a bunch of hobbies, running and biking, brewing, cooking, sailing in the summer, etc. I'm pretty good at the most of that stuff, need some help with the sailing though, or just someone else in the boat, it's pretty fun, we won't tip over much. I'm interested in a bunch more hobbies too, kayaking, working on my Spanish (that's totally a hobby), I do play some musical

instruments on occaision, and I would like to start drawing again (mostly figure) when I'm less busy (ie out of school!).

"My life has been interesting, I've been through some ups and downs (mostly ups so far, thankfully), I know what's important to me. I've travelled, lived in different countries for a bit, jumped in as many large bodies of water as I could (and skipped rocks in them, which is key). There's still a lot to do, and I need someone interesting to do these things with: a date for the symphany, someone to camp or tromp around in the snow with, maybe bike over to West Seattle eat cupcakes and jump in the Sound and laugh at all the weirdos, or check out that new Tom Douglas restaurant. I make it a point to get out of the country every other year or so as well, if you have any travel plans and are a pretty laid back and adventerous traveler. My cousin and bro told me to look into this service, that is what brings me here. Can money buy love? YES it can, and the cost is 60 bucks! right?? Drop me a line, at worst I could be good for a laugh."

Lessons: Although this fellow does a great job of giving an *extremely* thorough picture of what his life looks like, it is *so* thorough that it seems there is no place for a woman. Between all his activities, how would he ever find the time to date? He also suffers from spelling/grammar errors and lots of clichés ("I've been through some ups and downs"). He does do a great job of suggesting date ideas toward the end.

His profile needs to be overhauled so that he's not including every activity he's ever done. He needs to choose a *few* of his favorite things to include. Further, he needs to spend time to think about who he wants to do this all with, and add that to the profile also. That way, when she comes across his profile she'll say, "Oh, that sounds just like me! I better write to him right away!" As it stands now, his personality is almost too big. Most women would probably wonder after reading his profile, "Where do I fit into all this?" and might move on instead of writing to find out more.

Profile 5 – You Sound Great But...: *"So how does this work?... I'm a guy, looking for a gal. Not enough detail? Alright - well a good smile and pretty eyes are a great start. I'm pretty active and so I hope you are too... I want someone who enjoys getting out and being energetic and doing things with me - biking, hiking, skiing, running, even walking and talking - pretty much whatever you can throw an "ing" on the end of is good for me. I really am just looking for someone with whom to share life and have fun. I know that everything is 100% more fun when there is someone else involved. I am a cyclist/triathlete and if you are too, mad props! But it's totally not necessary. During the winter, I love hitting the slopes. And throughout the year I like playing in a local orchestra and doing a bit of woodworking. I do a bit of everything. =) Total over the top romantic evenings are awesome, I'll even cook and bring you flowers. But just as good are the lazy days just hanging out and doing nothing in particular... although if it's nice outside, I'll find it hard to stay indoors. I treat my family, friends, and loved ones like gold and will go out of my way to make people happy - I just get a kick out of it. I'm fairly grounded in my life, but like mixing things up and trying new things too. I like being excited by someone who surprises me and pushes new ideas into the picture. Spontaneity is always fun. I'm pretty easy going and usually find things in life to be really good."*

Lessons: This guy sounds great, but who is he talking to? He's done a good job of describing himself (although more concrete stories would be a nice addition), and even describes what he'd love to do in his free evenings or on a date. But what kind of lady is he looking for? His profile casts almost too wide of a net. If he added some greater detail about what he wants (e.g. someone to train for his next triathlon with) he could be weeding out less compatible matches and ensnaring just the right ones.

Profile 6 – They're Not Charging By The Word: *"Arizona native new to both the Seattle area and online personals. Attended college and started my career in the deep south. I am very excited to be back in a big city and meeting new people. In my spare time; I enjoy jogging, sports, traveling, hanging out with friends and anything for a laugh. Always looking for new fun/rewarding activities. Any recommendations?"*

Lessons: Is this dater looking for a relationship or a tour guide through the Northwest? In addition to having an incredibly generic profile, this is way too short and doesn't use complete sentences. She is missing some great opportunities to talk about concrete life stories that give us a glimpse of a real person behind the computer. She is also missing the chance to describe what she's looking for in another person. This profile could describe just about anyone and could be matched with just about anyone. The result? Lots of wasted time on poor matches!

Profile 7 – Too Busy For Love?: *"I am just a small-town girl looking to find the right balance in life.*

"I work a lot. Depending on the time of the year, I travel about 50% of the time. I am extremely driven and dedicated to my career. I try and find time to stop and smell the roses though too.

"When I am not working, I am usually laughing with friends, training for my next triathlon, cuddled up

on the couch watching football, spending time with my amazing family, or exploring the city.

"I grew up all over the country, but I spent the majority of my time in Wisconsin. The midwestern culture is still alive and well in me. I am VERY friendly and outgoing. I treat people like I would like to be treated, and I expect my partner to do the same."

Lessons: This woman did a great job giving true examples of what she enjoys in her free time (watching football, triathlons), but how much time will she really have for a relationship? If you have an unusual situation (like being gone 50% of the time) you have to work extra hard to let people know what a relationship with you would be like. Sell them on it even as a potential benefit (he'll still have plenty of time to spend with his buddies)! She could also improve her structure to talk about where she's from, what she does now (and how odd, but great it would be for a boyfriend), and what she's looking for in a man.

Profile 8 - The Cocky Kitchen-Sinker[37]:
"Howdy! I wish to find that special girl who shares my passion for life and my love of laughter. I actively engage academics, rock climbing, mountaineering, mountain biking, skiing, triathlon, running, weight lifting, and anything that requires the outdoors and enforces the individual spirit. I absolutely love my life, my family, friends, profession, outdoor pursuits, traveling, food and music - and of course God who has given me great ambition and opportunity. I recently obtained

---

[37] I saved the "best" for last. This epic essay was crafted by the first person I dated online. I can only say that I was 22 at the time and that I have come a long way since then. Incidentally, he had time for almost none of the activities he lists here (although he had done them all), and practically never saw friends OR family. And yes, he was EXACTLY as you would imagine based on this free-write.

my doctorate, led a climbing expedition to Patagonia, climbed many prominent mountains around the globe, skied Colorado and Montana, surfed and mountain biked across Hawaii, researched cardiac atrophy in astronauts for NASA at the Kennedy Space Center, launched an Atlas Rocket into space, worked in San Antonio, Denver, San Francisco, Seattle and rural Montana hospitals, delivered babies and performed surgery. I was in an earthquake, a hurricane, an erupting volcano, had alligator encounters in the Everglades, a bear scare in Yosemite and just finished my first triathlon 2 days after moving to WA. I demand much from myself so that I possess the character required to give that special girl and my family the best of everything. That is why I am looking for someone who meets challenges with wit and tenacity, achieves her dreams while having FUN in the process, and has strength of constitution. Someone who is high energy, loyal, optimistic, intelligent, loves the outdoors, traveling, kids, telling and listening to stories. I desire a friend who I can support, be there for and cook a fabulous meal for followed by a massage. She can teach me something she loves, help with a crisis workload, join me out on the town, give me a good massage and a quiet dinner at home, be there to listen, be a travel partner and a cohort in misadventure. This is a personal challenge. If you meet these criteria, we can go climbing, go for a ride, meet for coffee or spend an afternoon relaxing with friends."

Lessons: This is so far over the line between confident and cocky that the line has gone over the horizon and out of view. On the positive side, he paints some great visual images of things he's done, and sets forth very clearly who he's looking for. HOWEVER, it needs to be toned down about 75% in every way; he needs fewer superman stories and fewer demands from his potential date. This is not a competition to be crowned Captain America, you're just trying to meet a nice girl.

So now you have seen some examples of what works and what doesn't, and you have my seven rules to follow, so get in there and get started. Remember, don't post your profile until you've finished it and had it reviewed by someone else! If you need additional help crafting the profile, or want it professionally reviewed, we can help you write an essay that will wow the socks off Your Match at www.MeetYourMatchOnline.com.

Chapter 12:
Fixing Common
Profile Mistakes

We've already talked about a few common places that online daters go wrong – especially with photographs. But if you've cleared that potentially fatal hurdle and are even through your draft of your essay section, make sure you avoid these common pitfalls:

Mistake: Narcissism. Yes, your online profile should be about *you* and should let the reader get to know a bit about you. You are trying to market yourself to the right man or woman, after all. But as with all good marketing campaigns, you need to know your audience. If you spend the entire profile talking about how you've competed in 53 triathlons, wrestled alligators, worked as an ice trucker, and engineered the ceramic tiles for the last space shuttle (see "The Cocky Kitchen-Sinker" in the previous chapter), a potential date may end up feeling intimidated and unsuitable for you.

Suggested Fix: Tell your potential matches enough about yourself to get them interested and to give them ideas for conversation topics to talk about with you. However, make sure to also include a portion about what you're looking for in a date. Does she also need to love ice trucking? If he's only run 10K races, and doesn't know how to swim, is he out of contention? One fun way to accomplish this goal is talk about things you'd love to do with someone (keep it clean!). For example, if it's a big thing in your life, you can talk about how you'd love to have someone to train for an upcoming half marathon with. If you love to fish, say you'd love to show someone else how so you can have some company out in the boat.

Mistake: The Laundry List. In contrast to the Narcissism mistake, many online daters spend far too much time talking about what they "need" from another person. It's VERY important to know what you're looking for (you'll be a lot faster at finding it), but you don't want someone with great potential to have so many opportunities to say "Oh, shoot, I guess they're not looking for me because I only have eight of those ten traits."

Suggested Fix: Be open enough to allow the person to contact you so that YOU can weed them out, rather than having them self-select out. If you have any deal-breakers, you can set those out, but otherwise avoid creating a long list of faults or requirements. It could be that on the right head, you'll come to love brown/blonde/red/silver hair.

Mistake: Clichés! There is only one way clichés should be used in dating profiles: to be funny. Otherwise, there is just no place for them. Done right, you can use clichés to break the ice (e.g. in a joking way – "I love button collecting and underwater basket weaving") but done wrong, they can ruin a profile and make you come across as generic and bland. Common clichés include "enjoys long walks on the beach," "looking for my better half," "I like to work hard and play hard," "I like to have fun," and "I love to laugh." People often use them as a crutch to avoid having to be specific or clever. When you can cut these from your profile and replace them with true stories your essay will really pop!

Suggested Fix: Instead of using adjectives, tell about yourself using stories and vignettes. Instead of stating that you're creative and clever, tell a story about when your creativity and cleverness got you out of a tight jam (e.g. the time you were called to the neighbor's house to help free their child's head from between the banister using Crisco, floss, and a banana peel). Don't say you "love to have fun" – give a concrete example of what you like to do for fun in a free weekend (e.g. "on a Saturday you might find me out on the links or at the climbing gym").

I had one client who wrote about how much she laughs, and that she even laughs in her sleep. Not only did it show off what a happy person she was, it was something that nearly every man who wrote to her would ask about. You never know what little story will capture someone's interest. Specificity paints a great picture in your date's mind of the fun he or she will have with you when you finally meet.

Mistake: Writing a Treatise: Women tend to make this mistake more than men (men, incidentally, often tend to be too terse). Remember, you're trying to give the person a synopsis of who you are – just enough to make them want to read the rest of the article (i.e. meet YOU!). Don't try to force your whole personality at them all in an online dating profile. Two to three paragraphs is usually sufficient to let the person know a bit about you, what you like to do – or plan to do – with your life and time, and who you're looking for.

Suggested Fix: If you think you fall into this category, just remember less is more. We all like a little bit of mystery (which is why there are doors on bathrooms). Leave something to the imagination. If you're terrible at this, find a service like Meet Your Match Online that can review your profile for you or even help you write a completely new one. If you aren't willing to spring for professional help, enlist a friend or family member. They likely won't be quite as cut-throat (it can be hard to be totally honest with good friends) but they're better than nothing!

If you've already gone through the creation of your profile, take another look at what you've prepared (and maybe get another set of eyes on it) to make sure you don't fall into any of these categories!

PART FOUR: MEETING YOUR MATCH

In the final part of this book, you will learn what you need to know to take you from having a well-crafted profile to actually meeting great prospects *in person!*

We'll cover (1) how to write emails that will get a positive response, (2) proper online dating protocol (is there a place for chivalry online? How can you say no without being rude?), and (3) how to get beyond that first date to the second date and to a serious relationship.

Chapter 13: Writing Emails That Will Get A Response

After you've gone through all the work of determining who you want to date, choosing the perfect photos, and crafting the perfect profile to get you noticed, you need to make sure that you can reel in any great catches that you hook. After all, the key to having all your hard work pay off is actually *going on that first date*!

Not surprisingly, there have been numerous studies conducted addressing how to get your email noticed, and how to increase your chances of getting a response. I have gathered this information and condensed it in this chapter so you can put it to work for you!

The Subject Line:
Your Email's First Impression

We've already talked a bit about creating a good opening sentence or headline for your profile, but let's get down to specifics. It's amazing how a little tweak of a subject line can make a huge difference in whether your email gets a response. If you're feeling uncreative, then... well it's probably best not to send emails out at that time. BUT, if you do start sending emails out, and can't come up with something clever, at least go for "Howdy" instead of "Hi." Even better, try "How was your day?" An inquiry is more likely to get a response than a standard greeting.

A recent poll from OkCupid[38] showed that the average response rate to any given email is 32%. That is to say that if you write an email to someone, you only have a 1 in 3 chance that he or she will actually write back. You can boost your chances by using the right words to capture someone's attention. For example, emails containing the words, "how's it going" in their title got a 53% reply rate, whereas emails with the word "hi" got only a 24% reply rate – well below average. The lowest ranked standard greetings were "hi," "hey," and "hello." The highest ranked standard greetings were "how's it going," "what's up," and "howdy."

Even better than these standard greetings would be to reference your email recipient's profile, letting him or her know that you paid special attention to it, and that you're not sending around your usual form letter that you write instead of having to come up with new content. If he or she loves crosswords, try an enticing, "I do Sunday's in pen!" I had another client who loved to travel respond to a Match (who she's now happily dating) who wrote to

---

[38] http://blog.okcupid.com/index.php/online-dating-advice-exactly-what-to-say-in-a-first-message/

her with the headline "I have two passports!" He appealed to her interests and made it a riddle for her to figure out why he would have more than one passport. Making your headline unique is a great way to boost your chances of getting a response.

Email Content:
Word Choice

The content of the email, down to the specific words you use, will play a large role in whether you get a response – especially in whether men get a response from women. The big rule here is to *avoid commenting on personal appearance in your emails!*

OkCupid's research indicates that emails containing words referencing appearance or emails with sexual overtones are *much less likely to get a response* than emails containing words indicating your interest in the person's activities. My assumption behind the reason for this is that focusing on physical attributes makes the email feel more like a pickup line, and less like genuine interest.

When sending email to potential matches, the word "sexy" receives only an 18% response rate, whereas emails containing the word "awesome" received a 39% response rate (again, where 32% response rate is average). Other words to avoid are "beautiful," "hot," and "cutie." Words to incorporate and boost responses are "cool," "it's nice that..." and "fascinating." Similarly, telling someone "you're pretty" or using the words "very pretty" yield response rates well below average.

Other good words to use are words that indicate you're interested in learning more about the person. The following words and phrases yielded 10 – 17% higher than average response rates: "curious what," "your

133

name," "noticed that," "good taste," and "you mention." Showing that you've read his or her profile and are excited to learn more about him or her make people feel flattered and are a great way to start off getting to know each other better, which is the whole point, after all!

One single woman I know who is working hard to find love has a chest size that's quite a bit larger than average. She's gorgeous, has a beautiful daughter, and many wonderful things going on in her life. However, her biggest pet peeve with dating is that *so many men* ask about her bra size. Even those who don't ask via email end up making a comment or asking a question about it on the first date and she has taken to simply excusing herself from the date at that point and going home. When in doubt, stay away from commenting on someone's physical attributes, even if you think you're paying him or her a compliment; it might not come across as you intended.

Email Content:
What You Should Do

Be Upbeat and Positive. Just as you would in person, being upbeat and positive is a great way to attract people to you. Be bright, be pleasant, and people will want to know more about you. There's an old adage that *people will remember how you make them feel* much more than what you actually say. So send an email that brightens their day.

Don't Sink Your Own Ship. Many online daters make the mistake of leading with something that takes them out of the running before the gun even fires. For example, I received many emails that began "I know I'm out of your height range..." or "I know I'm too short for you, but..." Give the recipient the opportunity to decide for him or herself whether you're out of contention. Let him or her explore your profile and get intrigued by what you have there. After all, if you're writing then you probably think you would be a good match in spite of the dif-difference, so focus on proving that to the other person!

Be Specific. It is always a good idea – just as when writing your profile – to bring up specifics. Demonstrate that you read what the person you're emailing wrote, and that it made an impression. Show them that if you met in person you could discuss topics of interest together. OkCupid's study showed that bringing up topics like literature, physics, favorite movies, bands, and the like in an email yielded greater response rates than average – often 10% higher or more.

Be Honest. As in your profile, it's important to maintain honesty in your emails. Being consistently honest and genuine reassures potential matches that you are who you say you are – a good person, right?!

Be Kind. People often try to create a bond by uniting against a common enemy in a first email. They'll attack something, some school of thought, or even a specific public figure. While this kind of bonding can seem charming at first, it often leaves the reader with the feeling that the person they're communicating with is a negative person. This leads to the lingering concern, "How long until she turns on me with that acid tongue?" If you're trying to unite over something, pick something wonderful that happened. There's nothing like a good triumph of the human spirit to promote bonding and leave the reader feeling great.

Email Content: What You Should NOT Do

Get Too Personal. Be careful about becoming too personal too quickly. There's just something about

135

the perceived anonymity of email, texting, and instant messaging services that lends itself to people opening up too much or too quickly.

A good rule before you send an email out to someone you haven't met in person yet is to think about whether you would be comfortable with a stranger you just met on the bus reading the content of your email. As far as you know, the person's profile could have been completely fabricated. Be sparing with personal details or information until you are well into a relationship.

Use Too Much Shorthand. Stay away from too much shorthand. Think of your pre-date emails as an interview to get through. You'll want to continue checking your spelling and grammar, avoid use of emoticons and other shorthand, and generally put your best foot forward. Once I received am email from a suitor that said "How r u grrrrl? Get 2gether 2nite?" I just laughed and deleted it. I didn't even look at his profile. It's just so ridiculous (because he *wasn't* joking) that I couldn't take him seriously.

Be Thoughtless In Responses. Ripping off a quick email on your way out the door is not what you want to do to attract someone. A poorly thought-through email that mentions nothing about his or her profile – or worse, one that you copy and paste and send to everyone – is more likely to get deleted immediately than to get a response.

Long after My Match and I exchanged our initial emails, he told me how he wrote them. He would read through the email I had sent to him and brainstorm his responses. He would then handwrite his responses out and make sure they were organized and said what he wanted to say. He made sure that at the end of each paragraph he asked me a question about myself and invited

136

me to respond and share more. Once he'd drafted it, he would type it up, spell check it, and only THEN would he send it. And guess what? It worked – not only did I want to send him a response, but *boy oh boy did he stand out!*

Be a Master of the Obvious. My Dad always jokes about having his M.O. degree ("Master of the Obvious). Saying things in your email like "I'm trying online dating," or "I saw your profile," or "I thought I'd write to you," tend to yield a "no, duh" response from the email's recipient. These lines usually come out when you haven't taken enough time to study the other person's profile and see what you should really be writing about. Instead, try browsing their profile to find two or three things you have in common and ask him or her more about those. Once you actually put the email together, just get straight to these points.

Be Offensive/Sexual. Anytime you are crafting a first email, making your first phone call, or going on that first date, avoid potentially fiery topics like religion and politics! Although these issues may be near and dear to you, and although the way in which a date answers your questions about these topics may be deal-breakers for you, leave them for a later date. Find out whether you like your date *outside* of these issues first. Then, when you're both more comfortable, you can discuss these difficult topics. I recommend waiting because people often share more common ground than they realize, but aren't willing to have a deep conversation about sensitive topics until there's a comfort level established.

Similarly, avoid sexual topics at all cost. People who flatter too much or reference sexual topics are *far less likely* to get a response than those who stay away from those subjects. Additionally, bringing up sexual topics on a first date sends the signal that you're not interested in a long-term relationship, and you may find that the dates tend to get cut short after these topics are broached.

Get Too Excited About An Email. Finally, I'll remind you (especially women!) not to get too excited over a good email you *receive*. Not to burst anyone's bubble, but there are a lot of services out there that write all the emails for their clients (not mine, as I find that to be a deceptive practice). People also tend to fill in blanks with the rosiest picture possible (which likely would not be the true reality). The person with the silver tongue on the other keyboard may be a professional writer and not be the person you'll eventually meet. Also, remember that a lot of scams begin with AMAZING emails. An email is just a gateway to a phone call, which is a gateway to a first date. Wait to fall in love until you've met in person *at least* several times (I say this somewhat tongue-in-cheek, but it does happen that fast for some people).

Chapter 14:
Dating Etiquette
For An Online
World

When you've selected just the right dating service, when your profile is complete and loaded, and after your photos have been approved, you're ready to dive in. So now what?

Browsing

If you're on a service that allows browsing (most sites other than eHarmony and Chemistry) spend some time checking out others' profiles to get the lay of the land. (If you're on a service that doesn't allow browsing you may have to wait a day or so for your first round of matches.)

To get started browsing, get a few of your deal-breakers into the search engine feature of the site and go for it. Be aware that as you do this, though, that browsing can become overwhelming for certain daters. Putting in a search for men in my age range within 5 miles of my house (I live in a suburb of a big city) yields 2,000 matches (the search engine's limit). Yikes!

It can also be discouraging to spend a long time searching through potential matches and not find any- one. If you're starting to feel frustrated or discouraged that's a sure sign that it's time to stop for the night. Just step away from the keyboard and come back to it tomor- row.

If you're just starting out and don't know how much time you can handle or how much time you should be spending to get your money's worth, a good rule is to try to spend 30 minutes a day (or an hour every other day, schedule permitting) going through your matches or communicating with people who look interesting to you. If you don't interact with it, it's a lot less likely to be successful for you. Remember, the service leads you to water, but you're the one that has to decide to drink.

> *If you don't have the time or energy to put into searching, don't give up – just hire a service to do it for you!*

If you don't have the time or energy after a long day at the office to put into searching, consider using a service like Meet Your Match Online to do the targeted searching for you. My business will find potential matches for you and provide periodic reports of a select few people who actually meet your *true* criteria – not just what the online dating service thinks would work well. This way, you can put your time and energy toward emailing only matches with great potential.

Get the Conversation Started

For a long time in my dating life, I refused to initiate a communication through an online dating service. This "worked" for me only in that I was asked out by other online daters; it didn't work for me in that I wasn't able to meet My Match. The rules of online dating are slightly different than the rules in real life (at least the ones in my old-fashioned world) where the man should ask the woman out. It was only after I wised up and broke my own antiquated rule that I found My Match.

When you're dating offline, you meet someone face to face. It's generally obvious that you both see each other. You can assume then, if you talk to the person and get a chance to connect with him or her that if there's a spark someone (usually/hopefully the man) will make a move and ask the woman out. In contrast, when you see someone online, there is *no guaranty he or she sees you.* Just because you have come across the other person's profile doesn't mean they've come across yours. So, when it comes to dating online, if a woman comes across a man's profile and finds that she is interested in getting to know him better, *she* should express interest – even if just with a wink – in case he has not or will not come across her profile.

Many online daters choose their distance settings so that they're only looking for people within five to ten miles of their home. If you live in a big city, this can yield a tremendous number of search results, so many daters stop there. After all, it is so much more convenient to find someone who lives just around the corner. However, someone living farther away may have greater distance settings and may be able to see your profile, while you (with your shorter distance settings) would never be shown theirs, no matter how great a match you might be.

When it is the women who have the greater distance settings, if their rules are not to make the first contact they will *never hear from men* with smaller distance settings. *NEVER.* So women, if this is the case, it's imperative that you at least send a wink or short email to let him know you're out there and a potential great match for him. You can let him take it from there.

Just because a relationship starts out long distance doesn't mean it will always stay that way. When we first met, My Match lived 60 miles from me, and wouldn't have come across my profile, but as soon as I winked at him, he initiated email contact and we were off to a great start. After we started dating, he drove to see me several times a week and within 4-5 months of our first meeting, he moved to within 5 miles of my house so we could see each other more frequently and easily. When it works, you'll work it out!

Online Dating's Version of Chivalry

I struggled for a while with how to maintain the chivalrous world that I loved where men pull out your chair and open doors for you while dating online. Over time, I learned it can be done. Here are the guidelines to maintain the old-fashioned rules of chivalry in a new on-line dating world:

1. **Winking** (or other forms of non-email communication)

    a. <u>Women</u>: If you see a man you'd like to meet, send him a wink to let him know you're interested! You may not otherwise come up on his search results, so let him know you're out there. If you receive a wink from a man and you're interested, wink back. Let him do the work of initiating email communication.

b. <u>Men</u>: Winking is pretty weak. You are *much* more likely to get a response from a woman if you send an email. Take the time to look at her profile, and send a thoughtful email to show her you really care. She may get 20 winks a day and just skip those in favor of putting her attention toward men whose communications she views as more serious.

2. **Emailing**

   a. <u>Women</u>: I highly recommend letting the man send the first email. It may not be fair, but a woman who sends the email communication man may be perceived as desperate, and often compounds the problem by writing so much in a first email that she scares the man away. Let him make the first move and set the tone for the conversation.

   b. <u>Men</u>: If you're interested, send her a short email. Even a paragraph is fine. Just send enough to let her know you read her profile and why you're interested in learning more about her. A good way to do this is to pick up on something in her pictures that you enjoy (like "I see that you have a love of SeaWorld!"). A little humor is always a great addition.

3. **"Favoriting" Someone** (limited to certain online dating services)

   a. <u>Everyone</u>: Although being "favorited" can be flattering, getting "favorited" by someone who hasn't ever written to you or winked is just creepy. Save making someone a favorite until you're in frequent communication with him or her.

143

Deciding Whether to Meet

Dating online is a fun pastime for some people, a nightmare for others, and a time- and money-waster for the rest. However you feel about the browsing and pre-meet communications aspect though, it's critical to remember that it is *simply a means to an end*! The only reason to be on a dating service is to meet someone great and get out there and have a REAL long-lasting, loving, meaningful relationship. So don't spend too long online; just long enough to do your homework and see if any sparks might be there.

> *To make online dating work, you're eventually going to have to go meet in person!*

<u>Do Your Homework</u>. When you are ready to meet, and as you prepare, remember all of our tips about dating safety, and that what you've learned through the person's profile tells only a small part of their story – the part that they *wanted* you to see. Do your Google searching homework!

I've had some clients and friends ask whether you can go too far in researching your dates online. Possibly, yes, but sometimes that extra searching pays off. As a cautionary tale, one client told me about how she looked up the gentleman she'd been communicating with on the local court system's database. Lo and behold, she discovered that he'd been incarcerated for homicide (or was it only manslaughter...?). Not surprisingly, the gentleman hadn't disclosed this to her (maybe it's a third date kind of story), but she was shocked when she discovered his past (to put it mildly). The really sticky part of that situation was ending communications with him in a way that would avoid having him suspect she was on to his secret.

144

You can do background checks pretty easily online, and using the sex offender registry is free and can provide great information quickly. You may also want to check your County's database of cases to see if your potential date's name comes up. A small investment of time doing these searches can return a wealth of information you'll be glad you have!

Letting Him/Her Know It Won't Work Out. There comes a time in every online dater's life (usually quite early on) when he or she will receive a communication from someone who is just not a good fit. How to respond is the source of much debate. Here are my suggestions:

1. You need not respond to everyone who contacts you. If someone makes you feel uncomfortable, just delete the email and move on, or – if it's egregious enough – let the dating service know and flag the email for them.

2. If you get a "wink" or non-email communication, you need not respond.

3. If you receive a nice, thought-through email, it's polite to send back a response.

4. If you do respond and aren't interested, be kind and be brief. A simple "Thanks for your interest, but I'm afraid we're not a good match" works great. Something you've written yourself is always a bit nicer than the auto-responses provided by some dating services (even if the message is the same).

Setting Up a First Date

If things go smoothly and it looks like a first date is a possibility, you'll need to put some thought into who should initiate it and what to do. As you've already read,

I recommend that all my clients have *at least one* phone conversation before meeting in person.

Often you can learn far more about a person from the phone call than you did through reading his or her emails, especially nowadays when some dating services (e.g. businesses in big cities like New York and Boston) offer "ghostwriting" for clients. It may turn out that the person with whom you were corresponding is not the person you'll meet. A phone call is a good way to authentically speak to someone and see how the conversation goes. The call need not be so long that your phone battery dies, but rather just long enough to get those first jitters out of the way, see how they laugh and joke with you, and (God willing) set up a date.

I encourage my male clients to set up the first date. I'm just old-fashioned that way, and I believe it sets up a good dynamic in the relationship from the get-go by allowing the man to be creative and take initiative and letting the woman feel pursued and that she is desired.

If a couple who hasn't yet met is corresponding by phone and email and the man *won't* ask the woman out, I find that to be a sign that he's not genuinely interested. A man who is enthusiastic about a woman will generally waste no time in asking her out. However, when a man is hesitating in the online dating world, it's usually because he is pursuing other relationships he's more interested in, and holding her in reserve as a backup if those don't work out. There's a slim chance he's just trying not to come on too strong, but if the woman is letting him know she's available and interested in getting together and he's still not asking, I recommend that women move on to someone who is excited to get together.

The first date shouldn't be a huge production. Trying to force intimacy with a stranger by meeting over a romantic dinner *invariably* seems awkward. There's no reason to have a big romantic to-do with someone you've never met. Instead, think of something simple like a cup of coffee some weekend morning, or brunch at a bright, cheery restaurant.

For my first date with My Match, we met at a local coffee shop and went to walk around the local farmer's market on a sunny Sunday morning. The whole thing took just over an hour and we could have parted ways right then having had a great experience. We were enjoying ourselves, though, and planned on the fly to extend the date with a walk around the (very public – safety first) neighborhood and lunch.

Men, when you're planning, think of something short enough to escape quickly if it's a disaster, but at a place where you could extend the date if things are going well.

What to Do After the Date

You can learn a lot about how a date went from how it ends and what follows.

If the date went well: If the date has gone well, feel free to let the other person know at its conclusion. I urge men to talk first when parting ways after a date. If the man wants to see the woman again he can say, "Thanks so much for meeting me. I had a great time and would love to see you again soon."[39] If she responds positively,

---

[39] I acknowledge that this is a lot to ask, but clarity is the best policy here. You either enjoyed each others' company or you didn't. If you had a good time and she didn't, it's going to sting no matter what, but at least you'll know quickly and spare yourself getting more attached. And if you both had a good time, this is the best way to let her know you're interested, which is the best way to get another date!

you can even set up your next plans right then and there. However, if you get a lukewarm (or negative) response, don't push it.

You should not feel pressure to have some big romantic first kiss at the end of a first date either. After all, you're still practically strangers! Instead, if you're getting a good signal and are so inclined, see if he or she would be receptive to a hug. Plus, saving the kiss for the second or third date means and you'll be much more confident that it will be well-received. That confidence will be sexy and make everything a lot less awkward!

I find that men who have enjoyed a date will usually find some reason to call, or to send a text message or email later that day or that night, which is great. Something like, "Had a great time! Hope you got home safe." Ladies may respond in kind to a message like this. After a woman sends an email or calls (whether she originates it or is responding to him), an interested man should take the initiative to say "Great! I'd love to see you again." If both parties are interested, this is all that's needed to let each other know. It's perfectly all right for either one of them to plan the next date, although I advise women to *ask* if he would like her to plan something for them, or if he'd like to make the plans again. At least give him the option.

If a woman has not heard from a man, I recommend after a day that she call or email to let him know she had a good time. That's generally enough to let him know you're interested, and to open the door to a second date. I urge men who are interested to walk through the open door, although most *who are interested* don't need any urging.

I advise women not to strongly pursue a man who does not respond to her message that she enjoyed herself.

148

There's no reason to push hard for a second date if you're not getting a positive response. The reasoning is that men will often go along with a woman's request for a second or third date, just to see what happens, even if he's not that interested. Meanwhile, women become more emotionally invested, thinking the man is as interested in her as she is in him. LADIES, *if a man is interested, he will let you know.* Men generally aren't as complicated as we make them out to be.

If the date didn't go well: If you haven't had a great time, or already know you just aren't interested in seeing the person again, you don't need to imply (or outright state) that you would like to see him or her. A simple, "It was great meeting you. Have a safe drive!" is an easy way to escape the difficult conversation right then. Be nice and polite unless it the other person was a total monster to you and the date was a disaster.

Later that day, or the next day, it is polite to let the person know you aren't interested in seeing him or her again. If you've only had a first date, email is a fine (and often a benevolent) way to let the other person know you're not interested. Be gentle, be brief, and *be clear.* Let him or her know you had a great time, and that he or she seems like a great person, but that the connection you were looking for isn't there. You need not go into any great detail about your renewed longing for your ex, or the other person's flaws. Just let them know that it won't work out and wish them well in their future search. I have *never* had a gentle, brief, and clear email of this kind go poorly, and it is usually very well received and gets a nice response (even if it's just a "You too!").

> *When letting someone know you're not interested, be gentle, be brief, and be clear!*

Chapter 15:
How To Get A
Second Date

If you've written a fantastic email, had the great banter over your first phone call, and scored a first date, you're doing great! Keep in mind that the whole reason to do online dating is to get to the point where you're meeting in person! However, once you've put in all this work, you'll want to make sure you're presenting yourself well and giving yourself the best possible chance to convert this first date into a second, a third, a fourth...

Here's what you need to know to impress on a first date and to make sure you get a second one (if *you* want it):

1. **Be On Time**. Punctuality is a sign of respect. There's nothing that can get your date off to a worse start than being late. A friend of mine often said this funny line that stuck with me: "You can

always be un-early, but you can never be un-late."
I've remembered this when going to job interviews, dates, and appointments. I plan to be there 5-10 minutes early (or more if it's particularly important, or a location I've never been) and bring a book if I need to burn some time. If something comes up (like a major traffic back up for 10 miles) and you will be unavoidably late, CALL YOUR DATE and let him or her know what's going on. But do your absolute best to be on time, *especially* for that all important first date.

2. **Dress Appropriately For The Date**. Men are generally good at dressing appropriately for the date – often because they planned it! But here are some rules to play it safe:

   a. Never wear clothes with holes or stains *unless* the date is that you two are going to volunteer painting houses for charity;

   b. If you're going on a dinner date, wear something business casual. Ladies, you can also try that cute, but not-too-revealing cocktail dress.

   c. If you're doing something athletic, like a scenic bike ride, leave your fancy clothes and heels at home – wear shorts and a supportive top. If you both advertised yourselves as triathletes, you can even bring your *real* bike clothes instead!

   d. If he hasn't told you what you'll be doing on the date, ask for guidance on what you should wear to be best prepared for whatever he plans.

Show your date that you're up for what he planned. Being comfortable in your chosen clothes on the date will show in your confidence, and THAT is sexy.

3. **Eat Like A Human Being**. Not like a pig, and not like a bird. Bring your appetite, but don't come ravenous. Ladies, you don't need to break the bank if your date is paying for the meal (save the surf and turf for your dime), but do order "real" food. A side salad does not an entrée make.

4. **Act Like A Human Being**. Be open and friendly to your date and to everyone else you encounter during your date. Part of being comfortable and at ease on the date is remembering to be kind to waiters, hostesses, bike-rental guys, and valets. Seeing you act like a genuine, warm human being is always a quality your dates will enjoy and remember about you. That said, (men especially) make sure your eyes don't wander – and I think you all know what I mean – from your date. Being kind and respectful to others is important, but the one you should be pampering and focusing all your attention on is the one you came with!

5. **Stay Off Of Your Electronics**. In a recent survey we conducted of singles in the Northwest, one of the biggest complaints they had about first dates was if the other person couldn't seem to keep his or her hands off electronics (whether making phone calls, receiving – or sending – texts, reading email, or even browsing the internet). Taking time out for electronics (even if just to read a text) sends your date the message that you have better places to be or more important people to communicate with than him or her. In turn, keeping your focus on your date and silencing your devices lets your date know he or she is your top priority. And *that* is one message you *should* be sending!

6. **Be Casual And Relaxed... Not Vulnerable And Needy**. Be confident in who you are and what you have to offer someone. Let those qualities shine through. Even if getting married and having kids are critically important to you, don't discuss those topics on a first date. As a relationship develops between you, you will each begin to see a future together that appeals, which will organically lead to the topics of marriage and family. Trying to force these topics too soon just makes the other person uncomfortable.

7. **Use The Thanksgiving Rule**. Remember when your parents always told you to be on your best behavior when people came over? Remember being told at Thanksgiving to AVOID talking about religion with Uncle Ralph and DO NOT mention politics with Aunt Marie? Well the same applies to dates. These are critically important topics of conversation, but if you click with the person, you'll have lots of time to have these important discussions later. While you're at it, you should also avoid health issues, family issues, past traumas, exes, and sex.

8. **Don't Dumb It Down**. Men aren't usually the culprits here. They're happy communicating at their highest level, which is an excellent quality. Women, give men the same courtesy. You don't need to quiz them on the names of the Great Lakes, or the name of the 33rd President of the United States, but be yourself. If it isn't a match intellectually, you want to know that early on.[40]

---

[40] I understand that this can be very uncomfortable, especially when you're still getting to know each other. I've been on both sides of this; in the span of a few months I dated one man from Princeton who spent quite a bit of time explaining plasma physics to me and another who thought Australia was next to Ireland.

9. **Save the Drama for Your Mama.** No one –
   not men and not women – likes a lot of drama.
   Just as with baseball, there's no crying on first
   dates. Don't bring up topics that you're likely to
   feel very strong emotions about (exes, divorces,
   deaths in the family...). If you're at a loss for a conversation topic, take five minutes before your date
   to look online at some current light topics. What
   books are on the best-seller list? What movies are
   people going to see? Are there any exciting things
   going on in the sports world? (BONUS: These
   types of questions could lead to second date ideas
   like going to see a sporting event or movie.)

10. **ASK QUESTIONS**. If you're ever in doubt about
    what to discuss, *ask your date a question.* After
    all, you're there to learn about each other. "How
    was your day?" is always a good way to start. It will
    give him or her something to say, and you can
    latch on to one thing he or she mentions and relate
    to it. Perhaps the most important part of asking
    questions is asking *follow up questions.* When you
    ask to learn more about the topic, you're letting
    the other person know you've been listening and
    are engaged in his or her topic. Over the course of
    the date, try to find out about at least three things
    your date enjoys. Make sure to give him or her
    openings to ask about you too.

11. **Paying For The Date**. Men – pick a restaurant
    you can afford. There are some women out there
    (though not many) who will get the most expen-
    sive thing on the menu and then never be heard
    from again. Be prepared. If you can't afford some-
    thing fancy, then don't go somewhere fancy! If
    she's interested in *you*, she'll understand. If she is
    interested in a wallet, she can go find someone
    else's wallet. Even when the woman earns more
    she often wants to see the man at least make the

155

move to pay. Down the line in the relationship, if you both want to go somewhere fancy that the gentleman can't afford, the couple can discuss how best to handle that.

12. **Call Him or Her**. The final, perhaps most important, step in ensuring you get a second date is communicating with each other after the first. Nothing breeds insecurities faster than not hearing from the other person for a long time after the date. If you're into someone and NOT into playing games (just don't do it), let them know – within 24 hours, ideally. Just talk to each other and keep the good feelings going. If you're not hearing from each other for days after a first date, there's no surer sign that things are headed for trouble. If you aren't interested in seeing the person again, send him or her a short email to convey that and wish him or her luck in the future search for love.

With these tips under your belt, you're sure to get to that all important *second* date. It's a great achievement because the nerves on the second date are generally much more under control and you get a better chance to relax and let true personality shine through.

If you are having trouble getting to the second date or need additional coaching about what to do when you get one, you can sign up for date coaching with Meet Your Match Online, which offers subscriptions for unlimited monthly assistance by email or by the hour coaching over the phone or via Skype.

Chapter 16: Thriving In A Relationship

Many believe that the beginning of a relationship is the most magical time. You get butterflies just at the thought of seeing the other person, and the air is nearly electric with tension, excitement, and the anticipation of new love. While new love can be wonderful, I maintain that there's just no comparison to the feeling you get from the lasting, unconditional kind of love that comes from a long-term relationship.

If you're able to follow all the steps in this book, it won't be long before you find yourself setting sail on a wonderful new journey, your destination a trusting and loving relationship with the man or woman of your dreams. The course you set may not be the course you eventually follow, however. You may have stops and starts, course corrections, and certainly many learning opportunities. In order to thrive in your new relationship

157

with the skills you've now learned, you'll need to: (1) recognize a relationship that isn't right and avoid wasting any more time in it; (2) sense trouble early and either avoid it or bail out fast; (3) maintain your sense of self, your friendships, and your hobbies; and (5) learn to share your time, talents, space, and yourself with someone else.

Recognizing Bad Relationships

It's a lot easier than you might think to determine whether you are in a bad relationship. Until I met My Match, I had so much trouble figuring it out. I thought there was some big trick to this but it is actually *so easy*. Here's the key question to ask yourself at any given moment in a relationship: *"How do I feel?"* Do you feel happy? Secure? Reassured? Excited? Do you love the way you feel when you're with the other person? All of those are signs that you're in a good – dare I say GREAT – relationship. However, if your answers to this question are more along the line of "nervous, insecure, uncertain, tentative, unhappy, not sure where you stand, and suspicious," then you have a potentially bad relationship on your hands.

In a healthy relationship, you feel *better* being together. You are comfortable reassuring each other of your feelings – although not much reassurance is needed – and it is easy to communicate about how (and potentially where) the relationship is going. I remember a point in every bad relationship I was in when it started to feel like we were in a canoe going against the current, and I was the only one paddling. If I stopped for even a moment, we'd be forced backwards or flipped over. There was no teamwork, no opportunity to rest every once in a while, no thought that the other person was even participating in the relationship at all. Those were all important feelings to have, I just should have *listened to them!*

158

Sensing Trouble Early

At this point you understand the importance of *sorting* in finding Your Match, and you not only want to be able to recognize a bad relationship, you want to be able to recognize it FAST. Don't depend on the other person to know when things are wrong. Spot it yourself and end it! You can do this in a variety of ways.

First, look for the early signs of trouble:

1. If you go out on a first or second date and the other person doesn't call or return your calls with a reasonable amount of time (usually 24 hours, and no longer than 72 hours), move on.

2. If the early get-to-know-you conversations over the phone or on dates are overtly sexual in nature, or if you are pressured for a sexual relationship quickly, then the other person isn't in it for the right reasons. Move on.

3. If you sense that the other person is hiding things from you, more likely than not, he or she is. Regardless, it's not the sense of happiness and optimism you should have with Your Match, so it's not right! Move on!

Second, don't wait for the "Reverse Dump," which I also call the "Passive Break-Up." If you start to get the feeling that the other person has checked out, chances are you're already on your way to a breakup. Your boyfriend or girlfriend may be taking the coward's way out having already decided to end things with you but having not let you know.

Your significant other will frequently seem to be a million miles away; he or she won't return calls, and won't put in any effort to keep you around because – sur-

159

prise – he or she doesn't want you around! This passive tactic is incredibly common, as a person tries to avoid being the "bad guy" by getting you to break up with him or her. The bottom line is, if you're not getting happy, positive feelings from your relationship it is NOT Your Match.[41] Instead of waiting for things to slowly fizzle out or dissolve on their own, take the proactive step of ending things yourself. You will be glad you did, and happy you didn't waste one more moment on the wrong person.

Third, keep focused on what *you* are looking for. Remember, there are lots of great guys and gals out there looking for love, and if you're using the techniques in this book, you'll meet a lot of great people. How-

> *Keep your focus*
>
> *on what* YOU
>
> *are looking for.*

ever, they are NOT all going to be right for you. You're trying to find Your Match and having your goals and objectives handy before and after a first date can help you to recognize *fast* whether you're on the right track.

Fourth, don't date someone to be nice! As soon as we start seeing someone new (for any length of time beyond a first date) we often feel as though we owe the other person something. I often found myself realizing that a date didn't have many (or most) of the qualities I was looking for but I continued to date him because I felt *sorry* for him and because he was such a nice guy. Soon I realized that I wasn't doing either of us any favors by continuing a relationship I didn't believe had long term potential. I was just wasting my time and his time.

---

[41] This isn't to say that all relationships will have some hard times, but if the bad outweighs the good, that spells disaster. After all, dating is *easy* compared to a married life with kids, a mortgage, and other obligations. Be glad you're just dating and not married to the person and move on!

Finally, pay *very close attention* to what the other person tells you – especially early on. I find that men are generally quite up front with their intentions, and will actually come right out and tell you if it's bad news. Strangely, women tend to ignore these outright confessions to their peril. For example, I had ex-boyfriends say to me, "I'm only going to hurt you," or "You're too good for me," and even, "This isn't going to work out." In retrospect, they were all explicitly saying (as one man DID) "THIS WON'T WORK OUT." And with every single one of them, it didn't. For whatever reason they continued to date me even though they saw early on that it wouldn't work out.[42]

What throws many women off is that they think if the man really meant what he was saying, he would end the relationship. Sometimes they do. The best ones do. Other times they – having happily confessed their intentions – decide to stick around to see what they can now get out of the relationship. Women may read this as the men giving them a chance to change their minds, but it never works out that way – their minds are never changed. Regardless, if the relationship continues you can believe that they will absolutely follow through on their word to hurt you, break your heart, cheat, or whatever the confession revealed.

> *If a man actually tells you he's going to hurt you, or that it won't work out BELIEVE him!*

---

[42] I want to give these men the benefit of the doubt about their intentions, but I expect most of them were waiting around to see if I would sleep with them. I base my suspicions on the fact that once each of them found out I was saving myself for marriage, it was generally only a week or two until the relationship ended.

Once you finally find Your Match you will see that he or she will move Heaven and Earth to be with you. You would *never* hear Your Match say that he or she will hurt you or break your heart. You will see how they do everything in their power to deserve your love every day, and that trying to talk you out of loving him or her is the absolute last thing on his or her to do list!

Maintaining Your Sense of Self

We've all had a friend (or maybe have been guilty of this ourselves) who gets into a relationship and it's as if he or she has disappeared. Were it not for their frequent lovey-dovey posts on Facebook, you'd think they'd been kidnapped. There's no more sure-fire way to start breeding resentment toward your significant other than by sacrificing everything you love and everyone you care about for the relationship.

In a secure loving relationship, you know that you can take time with your friends and to do the things you love (e.g. photography classes, salsa lessons, poker night) without putting the relationship at risk. You should both understand that by taking responsibility to maintain your participation in the things that you love you are ensuring that you'll continue to be a happy and complete person.

If you find that your friends start to wonder aloud, "What happened to you?" "Where are you?" "Haven't seen you in forever!" then it's time to think about whether you've lost yourself somewhere along the way in your relationship. Part of learning to be in a couple is learning how to be *yourself* in a couple.

Part of learning how to be in a couple is learning how to be yourself in a couple.

162

One strategy you can try if you're having trouble with this is to go out on some double dates with other friends who are in couples. Being around an old friend will remind you of who you are and let you become comfortable merging your old single life with your new life with another person.

Sharing Your Life With Someone

There can be a thousand different reasons why it can be hard to share your life with someone. In the beginning stages of a relationship, sharing your life may just be sharing life stories and experiences – but even this requires a certain level of trust. Opening up to someone creates vulnerability, a feeling that almost no one enjoys. For better or for worse, there is no other way to forge a strong bond with Your Match than opening up and sharing difficult memories, childhood fears, and your dreams for the future. It has to be done.

Depending on what you're trying to share, you may need to take some time. A good place to start is to share the things that you really enjoy. Bond over the fun experiences first. If you love to dance, ask if your significant other would like to join you at your weekly drop-in salsa class. If you love photography, bring your cameras along and try a weekend photo-safari around your neighborhood. The best relationships are built on common interests, so invite the other person to share what you love and show him or her why you're so passionate about it.

At a certain point, it will be time to share difficult stories and memories from your past. Choose the timing of this carefully. If you can, wait at least a few months before sharing your deepest darkest thoughts and fears with someone. Let the relationship develop and don't force that bond if it isn't there. It *is* possible to scare the other person away if you try to force it too early. But follow your significant other's lead. If he or she shares something with you, you may find that you are ready to reciprocate after all.

If things progress well, you may even begin to consider sharing space (moving in together!). Although each couple's circumstances are unique, I advise couples to wait *at least* until they are engaged to move in together. I say this for several reasons: First and foremost, once you've moved in together, it makes things much more complicated if you decide it's time to break up. The result is that couples who *should* break up stay together *much too long* merely for convenience.

> *Once you move in together, breaking up becomes much more complicated.*

Also, if you've found yourself with a commitment-phobe (which you may not have known at the time you moved in together) then you've probably reached the end of the line in your relationship's progression. There isn't going to be a wedding, so now that you've moved in, that's the end of the story. Ladies, don't hold your breath waiting for that ring from the commitment-phobe; you're never going to see it.

If you do decide to move in together, it's a good idea to set some ground rules first. If you need things tidy and his or her idea of cleaning a toilet is flushing it, you're going to run into trouble unless expectations are clear. Sit down and have a discussion about finances, common expenses, cleaning responsibilities, laundry, having people over, noise levels, and anything else you can think of that you might have discussed with your college roommate freshman year (except for, maybe, sharing clothes). If you're going to end up together, you'll have to have all these discussions at some point anyway, so you might as well get things off to the right start and avoid anyone developing bad habits at the outset.

Though much of this can sound daunting, don't despair! I spent way too much time in my single life (having lived alone for seven years) worrying that it would be so hard having another person in my life – and in my home – once I was married. What I should have been focusing on was how much fun it would be to have my best friend with me every day! The dishes, floors, and house in general may get dirty a bit faster than it used to, but chores *fly* by with two people working together.

Despite the risk of pain, the risk of rejection, and the struggle to find Your Match, I can't urge you strongly enough to stick with it. Just like finding love, relationships can be hard work. However, you would have *no* hesitation to get started on the work set out in this book, or to put your heart on the line *every day* if you could spend even one moment with the feelings of joy and happiness that await you. So go get started – and don't give up! I promise you **IT IS WORTH IT!**

Conclusion

Are you feeling inspired yet? I hope that as you've been reading, your excitement has been growing. By completing the preparatory steps you've learned here – determining whether you're ready for love, envisioning who you're looking for, and creating some deadlines – you are well on your way to success.

My hope is that you will take everything you have learned and follow the steps to create a fantastic online dating profile and be one of the *wonderful* people out there looking for love. I'm always scanning the online dating services for potential matches for my clients and I'm sympathetic that the pickings can be slim. With these tips, though, your profile will truly shine among the rest.

The amazing love-filled life you have always imagined for yourself is within reach. It is yours for the taking as soon as you're ready. Are you ready? Are you *excited*? If you feel that fire lit under you, go get started *today*! Don't let one more moment get by without getting underway.

When you do find the love of your life – and you will – I hope that you will contact me to share the wonderful story of how you finally met Your Match. I'll be waiting to hear from you! Send me an email at: Laura@MeetYourMatchOnline.com.

Be Safe! Have fun! GET STARTED!

Special Free Gift #1 From The Author

A $150 Value!

As a reader, you can now get benefits previously available exclusively to clients of Meet Your Match Online! Visit our website to download and print the worksheets you read about in this book for FREE!

http://www.meetyourmatchonline.com/how-to-meet-your-match-online-bonus-material/

On this site, you'll be able to access both the **Recognizing Patterns Worksheet** and the **Identifying Your Match Worksheet**. Completing these worksheets will provide you with valuable insight into your own desires and give you a huge head start toward success.

The days of dating all the *wrong* people are finally behind you. After completing these exercises you will never again be stuck in long, fruitless relationships. You'll learn exactly what you want, and from all you've learned in this book, you'll know exactly how to get it!

Special Free Gift #2 From The Author

Become a member of an exclusive matchmaking service for FREE!

Mutual Friend
Intelligent Matchmaking

At Mutual Friend, our focus is on quality not quantity. We match our clients only when we believe there are common interests and a good base for a long-term relationship. We get to know our clients personally, and learn as our clients learn from their own dating experiences so that each match will be better than the previous.

To further our goal of providing all clients with *quality* matches, we don't accept just anyone into our database. All our clients have at least a college degree, and are looking for serious relationships. Visit the website today to learn more and sign up for FREE membership to date our clients.

www.MutualFriendMatchmaking.com

172

About the Author

Laura Henderson is a relationship expert living and working in Seattle, Washington. After graduating *summa cum laude* and *Phi Beta Kappa* with a degree in psychology, Laura graduated from law school with honors. She began her professional life as an attorney, working for several years in business, commercial real estate, and estate planning.

Laura began using online dating services in 2004 and has reviewed thousands of profiles over the years. Since 2006, Laura has helped friends, family, and even some of her business clients find love online.

After meeting her own Match online, and helping others find true love, Laura's passion for helping other singles find love inspired her to open her own online dating consultation business in 2011, Meet Your Match Online, and her own matchmaking company, Mutual Friend, both based on the fundamentals she learned that consistently lead to success finding love online.

Her background in psychology and legal training in writing make her uniquely qualified to understand the needs of her clients, conduct personal interviews to get right to the heart of their dating issues, and to assist them in crafting the perfectly worded profiles to get them noticed by *just* the right person.

To find out more about Laura and her business visit
www.MeetYourMatchOnline.com.

15632764R00099

Made in the USA
San Bernardino, CA
02 October 2014